The
SCOTTISH

Football Book

No. 19

The
SCOTTISH
Football Book
No. 19

Edited by

HUGH TAYLOR

STANLEY PAUL
London

STANLEY PAUL & CO LTD
3 Fitzroy Square, London W1

AN IMPRINT OF THE HUTCHINSON GROUP

London Melbourne Sydney
Auckland Johannesburg Cape Town
and agencies throughout the world
First published 1973

*This book has been set in Baskerville, printed in
Great Britain by offset litho by Flarepath Printers Ltd.,
St Albans, Herts. and bound by
William Brendon of Tiptree, Essex*

ISBN 0 09 117200 4

Contents

The Editor says . . .

A WARM welcome to all readers, old and new, to Scottish Football Book No. 19.

Season 1972–73 saw the centenary of the Scottish Football Association. A hundred years of football! It seems a long time. But—do things change all that much? Sometimes I wonder.

The finish of the season was exciting. Under the wave of hysteria which marked Celtic's eighth League flag triumph and the comeback of Rangers, however, there is still a great worry about the future of our national game in this country.

Once again the Old Firm dominate. There was a brave challenge from Hibernian—but it didn't last. Aberdeen failed to maintain the fine professional form of recent years. We all hope, of course, that these two clubs will soon be making the Scottish First Division a really *competitive* competition. The failure of Hearts, Dundee and one or two others of whom we expected better things is, though, a continuing disappointment.

Still, it's as well we do have the old Firm. Many of my readers moan that too much space is given to Glasgow's Big Two, that other clubs would flourish if they, too, were given the reams of publicity devoted to the green and the blue.

I doubt it. The Old Firm have the support because they are successful. If it weren't for them, we would be no more a force in football than Ireland, Malta or Luxemburg.

Don't blame the media for the wane of interest in other clubs. We in Scotland still hide our heads in the sands. We still continue to think we are living in the days of good Queen Victoria.

It is easy, of course, to put the blame on officialdom—and too many critics like to snipe at the ruling bodies.

The SFA and the League do their best. In these modern times, football must go deeper than their officials to find a remedy to a malaise that appears to afflict practically everyone except the top four or five clubs.

The time has come for streamlining. I know I've said this until you're probably sick of it. But it's the only answer. Scotland cannot support all the clubs who want a place in the sun. Smaller leagues mean richer clubs, better teams—and stronger competition.

You can suggest all the plans you like. Streamlining is the ONLY answer.

Football will survive, however. It is still a wonderful game, a fascinating sport. And Scotland continues to produce outstanding players.

Let's hope our clubs do better in Europe in 1973–74. Europe's the big one. Europe is where the glamour lies. And once again Celtic and Rangers are our main hopes.

When other clubs are winners as often as the Old Firm, then their support will flock again. And they'll get all the publicity they want . . . !

It was sad to see great old clubs Airdrie and Kilmarnock fall into the Second Division—but good to welcome back Clyde and Dunfermline Athletic.

As you'll read in this book, football is for everyone, about everything, the game we in Scotland still love most, whether we support Rangers or Forfar. I've tried to make this a SCOTTISH book. If there's an awful lot about the Old Firm, it's hardly my fault. The Old Firm are practically all Scottish football has to boast about. So, Hibs and the others, how about trying to change it? Hibs, I must say, tried so hard. I reckon they're the coming team.

HUGH TAYLOR

Old Firm drama

The great race for the Flag

THE delirious fans in the green and white favours, singing and dancing in the sober old streets of Edinburgh on the glorious evening of 28 April 1973, probably summed it up best.

Parodying a chant which had become a popular song, they sung: 'Hard luck, Wallace, Hard luck, son, Hard luck, Wallace, we've won another one.'

Indeed they had. Their team, Celtic, had just won their eighth successive League Championship by defeating Hibernian in the last game of the season at Easter Road. They were happy.

But there was probably even a little sympathy for Rangers as they sang. For the Ibrox team, under the driving command of manager Jock Wallace, had fought mightily to try to pip Celtic for the flag.

In vain. Rangers finished a point behind their oldest rivals.

What a nail-biting finish to an astonishing League campaign it was. Saturday, 28 April, was probably the most dramatic D-Day football has known, certainly the most decisive day since Kilmarnock beat Hearts 2–0 on their own Tynecastle in 1965 to take the title on goal average.

Ironically, Kilmarnock were also involved—and this time the last League match for them proved fatal . . . for they could only draw with Falkirk and go down,

while Dumbarton, celebrating their centenary, stayed up by scoring a magnificent win over Dundee United.

Celtic's great feat was the talk of football all over the world. No wonder. It was due, as manager Jock Stein said with a smile, 'to the fact that class will tell'. And it seemed that Parkhead had taken a monopoly of League flags.

But Rangers, also 100 years old, had given Celtic the fight and the fright of their lives.

In dreary November, however, there was no sign that Rangers were going to be the hunters.

Rangers were struggling yet again. Results were dreadful. The supporters muttered and jeered. 'We'll be in relegation trouble not chasing Celtic', they complained.

Rangers lost silly points. They had been disgraced in the League Cup, having lost to St. Mirren and Stenhousemuir. They could not find their way in the championship.

But Jock Wallace had faith. He reminded his players of their heritage, their traditions. He drove them mercilessly. He told them they could be a proud team again.

Gradually, Rangers believed in themselves. Gradually the fans began to cheer not sneer. Skipper John Greig drummed

on his men on the field. New boys like Tom Forsyth, Quintin Young and Tommy McLean gave the side a fresh look.

On 2 December, though, there was a disaster. Rangers were all over Hearts at Ibrox. But Hearts won 1–0. And Rangers became really angry.

That was the start of their greatest revival. They hit a brilliant winning streak. From that sad day in December to the end of the season, they did not lose a League game. More . . . they made a hit in the Scottish Cup. And, even better for their morale, they put up a splendid show against the world club champions, Ajax of Holland.

Rangers were back, really back, playing with all their old determination, allying superb fitness to glimpses of outstanding skill.

Suddenly, the whole League picture changed.

Celtic were, it seemed, out on their own. Their main challengers were Hibernian.

'Gr-eight, it's Eight for us.' That's what the happy Celtic players are saying as they do a lap of honour around Easter Road after beating Hibs to win the League title for a record eight times in a row.

The victory smile—from Celtic manager Jock Stein

And the buzz was that the match between Hibs and Celtic at Easter Road on the last day of the League campaign would settle the destination of the flag—for either Celtic or Hibs!

Then—sensation. Celtic faltered. Manager Jock Stein became ill. Influenza struck the staff. Other players were injured. Celtic lost their rhythm.

The grins disappeared from the faces of the Parkhead faithful. They saw their lead at the top disappear. There was a disaster against Airdrie and points were lost against East Fife, Partick Thistle and Dundee United.

Hibernian, too, began to struggle. Injury and suspension took their toll. Manager Eddie Turnbull's boys lost their touch.

And Rangers were the name on everyone's lips.

The change at the top had been swift. On 2 December 1972, Celtic led with 25 points, Hibs were behind them with 21 and Rangers following on with 18 points.

By 4 March, the positions were transformed. Rangers led with 41, Celtic were a point behind and Hibs had dropped out of it with 37 points.

Celtic, however, were not dismayed. Stein came back. So did players who had been off with injuries. And they finished like the true champions they are.

They took a blow at Tannadice where Dundee United held them to a 2–2 draw. After that, though, it was glory all the way. With Alistair Hunter bought from Kilmarnock to become a new Ronnie Simpson in goal, Celtic took new heart—and played magnificent football.

In their last seven League games, they scored 23 goals for the loss of only one. In between, they beat Dundee and Aberdeen in cup-ties—without Hunter having to bend to pick the ball from the net.

It was going to be the tightest finish in history . . . between Celtic and Rangers.

Would it all depend on the last day?

Up to a point. For on 21 April, Rangers' bogy team, Aberdeen, struck again. The Dons, for once out of the title chase, hit back like the great team they can again become, and held Rangers to a draw.

Indeed, they were the only team in the League to take points from Rangers from December to the end of the season, drawing both at Ibrox and Pittodrie. And how precious these lost points would have been to Rangers.

The position changed. Now Celtic

needed only a draw at Easter Road to retain the flag.

Rangers went into battle against East Fife at Ibrox, all out for a convincing victory—and hoping Celtic would lose to Hibs.

At Easter Road, however, Celtic proved themselves yet again. Hibs fought fiercely. But Celtic weren't content to hold them. They played a beautifully-honed, professional game, wore down their opponents and finished worthy champions with a 3–0 win.

With more than 20,000 delirious fans acclaiming Celtic's great feat, the players ran to the centre of the field to take a deserved bow. The fans weren't satisfied— so the Celtic stars found new stamina to make a victory circuit of Easter Road.

Certainly it was a wonderful way to win the title—for the game had everything: atmosphere, pressure, tension—and bouts of splendid play.

Rangers did beat East Fife. Alas, their splendid title challenge was in vain. But the Ibrox fans, too, paid vocal tribute to the boys in blue who had brought the magic back again to Ibrox, if not the title.

Just as dramatic was the battle at the bottom. Kilmarnock and Dumbarton had home games to complete their programmes. Victories were essential.

There was bad news at half-time for Dumbarton at Boghead. They had missed a penalty against Dundee United and they were winning only 2–1. Then they heard Kilmarnock were 2–0 up against Falkirk at the interval.

Dumbarton had the great fighting hearts. They put in a tremendous finish to win 4–1. Poor Kilmarnock collapsed in the second half and could only finish with a

'Hard luck, lads,'—that's what East Fife's Clarke says to Rangers players as they come off, rather dejectedly, after the last League game of the season. Rangers won and they had fought hard—but all in vain. They lost the title to Celtic.

2–2 draw. That put them into the Second Division along with Airdrie.

It was D-Day for dejection at Rugby Park, D-Day for delight at Boghead.

So an engrossing season finished with these honours—and disappointments. The line-up for season 1973–74 was:

European Cup — League champions Celtic. European Cup-winners Cup — Rangers. UEFA Cup—Hibernian, Aberdeen, with Dundee standing-by. Texaco Cup — Dundee, Ayr United, Dundee United, Motherwell, East Fife and Hearts. Stand-by team: St. Johnstone.

No smiles on the face of Kilmarnock manager Walter McCrae as he leaves the pitch after the last game of the season at Rugby Park. Killie had drawn 2–2 with Falkirk—and so they were relegated to the Second Division.

Promoted—Clyde, Dunfermline. Relegated—Airdrie, Kilmarnock.

It was a season to remember. And the top honours went to Celtic. Manager Stein summed it up like this:

'We won without having to rely on goal difference and I think that the way our team got over a sticky spell and did so well in the last game shows that class will tell.'

And he gave a warning to the other challengers: 'I expect Celtic to be even better next season for we will have matured and we will also have at least one new face.'

Jock pinpointed the spell after New Year as the time when he felt his club might lose the title. 'I had visions of the flag slipping away because we began to drop stupid points.'

How do Celtic do it? What is their success formula? Says Stein: 'We take every season, every game as it comes. We don't think about titles or honours, we just think about the game in hand.'

Celtic, of course, combine better than anyone the old with the new, the elegance of yesteryear with the method of today. They also have what appears to be a bottomless pool of outstanding players.

And they have Stein, the master tactician.

Rangers took praise for a terrific fight—but probably the club the neutrals sighed for was Hibs.

The Easter Road club ended the season with two trophies, a guaranteed place in Europe, a high position in the League and the satisfaction of having played brilliant football at all times.

They were, however disappointed. Manager Turnbull explained it like this: 'We had our sticky spell at the worst possible time. Right at the end. You can recover from a bad start and you can drive your way through a sag in the middle of the season but when it happens in the run-in you are in trouble.'

Probably Hibs began to fade when John Brownlie, then Scotland's most exciting player, broke his leg. Alec Edwards, another key-man, was suspended. And Pat Stanton, greatest of them all, lost some of his form.

Hibs' youngsters did well—but they couldn't last the hot pace and in one distressing week the pride of Edinburgh went out of Europe and lost to Rangers in the League. Suddenly Hibs were not involved —and so there was a slump.

Next, full-back Eric Schaedler was hurt and goalkeeper Jim Herriot lost his confidence.

Hibs were out of it. But they promise so much—and they had given fine entertainment.

Certainly Scotland need all the challengers the League can muster to try to stop the brilliant Celts running off with their ninth flag in a row.

Hunger the spur on a Royal Rangers occasion

THEY like to think of themselves as 'Royal' Rangers, the glamour club of Scottish football, the team with the Midas touch.

They are as tradition-conscious as Eton or a crack regiment.

But the crown had slipped, the purple had faded. Celtic had taken over as the kings of Scottish football. Rangers were hardly even crown princes.

Until the afternoon of Saturday, 5 May 1973.

That was the most important date for years in the long, illustrious Rangers' history. That was the day that Rangers became 'Royal' once more.

That was the day of the Scottish Cup Final, a gala as well as a royal occasion, with the charming Princess Alexandra at Hampden—the first time royalty had graced our national final—to see Rangers and Celtic in action.

The fans in blue were optimistic. The week before they had seen Celtic pip their favourites to take the League title yet again. But there was new faith in the side, who had recovered from a tragic start to feature in one of this country's longest un-beaten runs, new faith in iron-man manager Jock Wallace—and hope that the club must win a major honour in their centenary year.

Nevertheless, Celtic were favourites in the eyes of the bookmakers. They had found their old form, just won the championship and appeared to many to be the more confident, more relaxed side, with Rangers growing anxious as the big day neared.

The goal that won the Scottish Cup. Rangers' Tom Forsyth jabs the ball over the line to make the score 3–2 at Hampden.

To the neutral, the result was, as always in an Old Firm encounter, balanced on a razor's edge. It could go any way, a slip or a touch of genius making all the difference. Celtic were probably the better football-playing side—but Rangers looked on themselves as almost invincible, not having lost in their past 25 outings. Their spirit was tremendous, their pace fantastic, their morale sky-high.

And they had a terrible yearning for success, a hunger for a trophy to adorn a barren Ibrox cupboard and many people felt Celtic's challenge for a third Scottish Cup win in a row did not match Rangers' resolve to regain a slipped status symbol—a top honour.

The weather was in Rangers' favour and a wet, grey day made Hampden once again an imposing football fortress, out-dated, perhaps, but a symbol of our national game, harsh, grim maybe, but a stadium dedicated to football not carnivals or circuses.

Princess Alexandra, in navy blue, and her husband, Mr. Angus Ogilvy, received a warm welcome from the 122,714 fans and the atmosphere was electric as the teams lined up like this:

Rangers: McCloy, Jardine, Mathieson, Greig, Johnstone, MacDonald, McLean, Forsyth, Parlane, Conn, Young. Sub: Smith.

Celtic: Hunter, McGrain, Brogan, Murdoch, McNeill, Connelly, Johnstone, Deans, Dalglish, Hay, Callaghan. Sub: Lennox.

Referee: J. R. P. Gordon, Newport-on-Tay.

And what a marvellous show to set before a princess this final turned out to be, a right royal display, as dramatic a game as Hampden has seen.

The opening was predictable. Rangers stormed into the attack but Celtic were more subtle. And it seemed that the Ibrox dream was to be shattered yet again when

A Royal occasion at Hampden. Smiling Princess Alexandra talks to Rangers players.

Celtic opened the scoring in the 24th minute with a memorable goal, a goal which revealed in all its glory the splendid touches which had taken the Scottish champions to their record eighth title in a row.

Dixie Deans, hero of the previous season's final against Hibernian, made it with an accurate pass. The striker turned the ball past two opponents and Kenny Dalglish had read the move perfectly. The youngster ran on, held off defenders who turned too late and hooked a cool shot past Peter McCloy.

It was a goal that would have taken the heart out of most teams. But not out of Rangers. As the Celtic fans turned their end into a rainbow of green and white, skipper John Greig rallied his men and, with monumental effort, set about wiping out that lead.

Rangers' work-rate was astonishing. In midfield wee Alex MacDonald matched Greig in industry. Wingers Tommy McLean and Quintin Young stayed wide, inviting the pass, then dropping the ball in front of Alistair Hunter, the Celtic keeper playing in his first Old Firm match.

Now the match had assumed the pattern that was to continue to the end. Rangers had the hunger of a Benny Lynch, Celtic had the casualness of seasoned campaigners, permanent winners.

There was all the determination in the world in the foray of MacDonald in the 34th minute . . . hardly any in the tackle of George Connelly, prince of elegance, who didn't put his full weight into it. The Ranger crossed and again it was a boy in blue who rose most purposefully for the ball. Derek Parlane got his head to the cross and the ball flashed into the net for the equaliser.

That goal, naturally, spurred Rangers—but it also made Celtic become more menacing. And the final had champagne touches, fierce conflict and dramatic moments.

Incident followed incident . . . great players emerged, the poised Bobby Murdoch, the dashing Parlane . . . tempers rose sometimes . . . but the crowd loved it all.

Both sides made penalty claims—and didn't impress the referee, fussy but keeping a firm grip on the game. McLean was booked and later on Parlane, Connelly and McNeill also joined him in the notebook.

It had been a grand first half, with the honours even. Bigger thrills were to come after the turn-round. And what a start—for Rangers!

Hardly a minute had gone when the power and pace of the Ibrox team told. Chinks in the Celtic defence were shown as the thrusting Alfie Conn took the ball as it broke to him after an aerial duel between Parlane and McNeill. The Ranger ran on quickly, too quickly for struggling Celtic defenders who tried in vain to catch him. Out came the despairing Hunter. But Conn beat him easily and Rangers were ahead.

Celtic weren't champions for nothing. Rangers pressed harder but Celtic turned on the style in this astonishing final. Their old-time flair emerged at last and Rangers' defence was torn apart. A magnificent move in 51 minutes saw Dalglish, Johnstone and Deans in splendid action. Deans's shot was a scorer all the way—until John Greig dived across the line like a goalkeeper to punch the ball past the post.

Penalty. No doubt about that. And no doubt about the way the calm George Connelly stroked the ball past McCloy, moving in the other direction.

Two–two. Could Rangers survive now? For a spell it didn't look like it. Jinky Jimmy Johnstone gathered a Dalglish pass, took on McCloy, lobbed the ball over him, ran on and cutely placed the ball in the net. It was a wonderful piece of football—but a linesman had waved his flag for offside and the referee said No goal.

A blow indeed for Celtic—and there couldn't have been much in it. Still, the decision gave Rangers fresh hope and energy.

(*Overleaf*) The start of the winning goal. A header from Derek Johnstone hits the post. Then it runs along the line. You see Tom Forsyth, the man who scored, running in to get to the ball. (*Right*) A happy moment for Celtic. George Connelly scores from a penalty.

They moved into attack again and the Celtic goal now bore a charmed life. McDonald cleverly headed a Jardine cross —only to see the ball rebound from the post. Parlane missed a chance. And Rangers were keeping Celtic firmly penned in their own half.

Forsyth and Johnstone joined in the attacks. And again bad luck hit Celtic. Jim Brogan, that doughty left-back, was injured and had to hirple off. On came the speedy Bobby Lennox. But before the Celtic defence could reorganise, before Davie Hay could really take over in defence from Brogan, Rangers had scored an amazing goal—and won the Scottish Cup.

Derek Johnstone got his head to a McLean free-kick. The ball hit the inside of the post and ran agonisingly and slowly along the line. All on his own was Tom Forsyth, for there was no Brogan to cover the far post. He could hardly believe his eyes and he ran forward, unchallenged, to tap the ball a few inches over the line.

And that was that, though there were still thrills to come as Celtic tried to equalise.

But the goal by Forsyth, the sweeper who had never played in a losing Rangers side in a competitive match since being transferred for £40,000 from Motherwell in October, was the one that won the cup.

This is what he said about his first-ever goal for Rangers: 'When the ball came along the line, I thought it was going in. Then I saw it hit the other post and I was so excited that I nearly missed it. But I managed to stab it over the line.

So Rangers won 3–2 and deservedly took the cup, a trophy which had eluded them since 1966.

It was a wonderful night for Jock Wallace, who had won his first major honour in his first season as Ibrox manager.

Once again Celtic failed in their bid to win three Scottish Cups in a row. But, then, they didn't have that hunger of famished Rangers . . . and that was the real spur to the Ibrox success.

What a season it was

The sad sag

THE saddest aspect of the exciting race for honours which marked the end of season 1972–73 was that the name of Aberdeen was missing from the main action.

Everyone in Scotland had sympathy with the Dons, who had been in recent years the most consistent challengers to Celtic. For they were forced to transfer stars and were badly hit by injury.

They were still one of the best teams in the First Division, but they toiled behind the leaders—and that wasn't a happy position for the men of Pittodrie who had been so near top success when all others had failed in face of Celtic's supremacy.

Manager Jimmy Bonthrone summed it up when he said: 'Frankly, we knew we had lost any chance of winning the League away back in December. But everything went wrong. Henning Boel walked out, Willie Young took a nasty leg injury and Davie Robb had to undergo a cartilage operation.

'Then Joe Harper was sold and so our team were wrecked. So I had to make a big decision. I had to abandon hope of challenging for the title and start to build a new Aberdeen.'

The Pittodrie manager is adamant that Aberdeen were forced to sell Harper, the leading scorer who went to Everton. 'Once Joe was in the Scotland international pool the writing was on the wall as far as we were concerned,' said Jimmy sadly.

And Bonthrone is not the only Scottish manager who hates the thought of one of his stars joining the international squad.

Usually, it means a transfer request for the Anglos talk of the big money to be earned in the south, give the home Scots an inferiority complex and, unwittingly or not, hasten the demand to join the Saxon Klondike.

However, things should look up for the Dons soon. Boel has returned from Denmark, Young and Robb have recovered from injury and though others may seek transfers there are plenty of able young men to make soccer as well as oil boom in Aberdeen.

Mr. Bonthrone is enthusiastic about the promise of Billy Williamson and Joe Smith and he has also done a fine stroke of business in transferring the sturdy Eddie Thomson from Hearts to strengthen the Pittodrie defence.

Perhaps his ace is the famous Hungarian Zolten Varga, taken right to the hearts of the Northern fans because of his silken play. So graceful on the field, Varga has been described as a cross between a gymnast and a ballet dancer. Not surprising, really, Zoltan practises both arts.

For instance, he spends half an hour in the gym before a home match doing ballet movements. He reckons it's the only way to prepare for a game, for he insists it's essential to warm up and have the muscles supple before the kick-off. He adds rather ruefully: 'In Hungary and Germany, where I have played, no team would dream of going on to the field without this type of work-out. It's even more essential here, for it is so cold in Scotland the danger of

23

All happiness is there. Rangers manager Jock Wallace and his players after the final whistle.

Celtic were Aberdeen's bogy team—and paid a big part in the Don's sag. For Celtic beat the Dons in the Drybrough Cup

a pulled muscle is always there unless you are warm.'

What may put the Dons right back at the top is the fact that manager Bonthrone is remodelling his team on his own lines. Look out for the Cocks of the North really crowing again soon.

at Parkhead after extra time. They beat them in the League Cup semi-final at Hampden by 3–2. And they beat them 1–0 at Pittodrie with a late goal in the Scottish Cup quarter-final, after Aberdeen had forced a replay. Not much in it—but enough to dump the Dons. In this picture, you see the Aberdeen defence, with giant Willie Young on the ground, foiling a Celtic raid.

The curse of Scotland

THERE is no doubt that one of the curses of Scottish football is the transfer market. Almost since the dawn of the game, envious eyes south of the border have been cast on the fine players produced in the north. Around the turn of the century, many English teams had staffs almost 100 per cent Scottish. It's as bad today. No sooner does a Scottish club find and groom a star than English clubs are hovering around the door-step.

Fans are almost reconciled to seeing their favourite players go south—almost. They're angry when they read the transfer headlines but they know there's little they can do about it. For it's a vicious circle. The clubs are blamed for lusting after the Saxon gold. But the truth is that the clubs, with supporters leaving practically every season, need the money to survive. And there's the player's point of view. How can you blame a young man earning perhaps £50 at the most wanting to join an English club who will raise his salary to about £200 a week?

Last season, the Old Firm—who have taken more than their share, perhaps, of the best talent from other Scottish clubs— were involved in the transfer market. But they're luckier than most. They have splendid reinforcements. Celtic let Lou Macari go to Manchester United—and hardly missed him. Rangers earned big money from transfers of Colin Stein to Coventry and Willie Johnston to West Bromwich Albion—and became an even greater force in Scotland.

The fans of other clubs had reason to moan, however. Everyone seemed to be involved, from Dundee and Aberdeen to Dumbarton.

Frankly, I thought the transfer market

GONE . . . buzzing Lou Macari, Celtic's Scottish internationalist, was a big money transfer to Manchester United

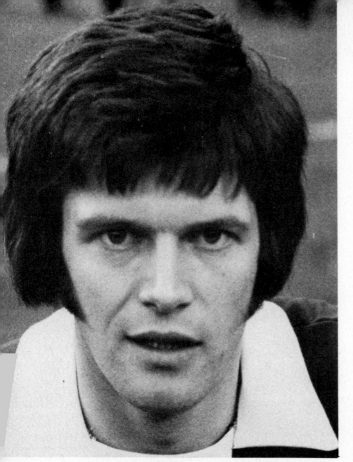

GOING . . . Dundee's goal-snatching centre-forward John Duncan was being watched at the end of the season by several English clubs—and seemed destined to move.

. . . Manchester City bought Rodney Marsh from Queen's Park Rangers. The London club could hardly wait until they bought a replacement—Stan Bowles, from Carlisle United. And that's when Scotland lost a star. Carlisle bustled north and bought Ken Wilson, Dumbarton's striker.

It is time the system was slowed if not halted.

Perhaps we're lucky in Scotland. We always seem to find brilliant youngsters, who come along on an endless belt. Nowadays, however, they are not being given time to mature, to settle before the English are buzzing around—or the lads themselves are dazzled by the thought of gold.

Isn't it peculiar, however, that the English keep telling us how superior they are, how much more competitive their leagues are, how much further advanced they are in style, coaching and technique?

Why, then, do they have a season ticket to Scotland—to snatch our best players?

We should take an example from some of the Continental countries, particularly Italy, where players can be bought and sold only during the close season.

The find

THE new hero of Ibrox is young Derek Parlane, fast developing into one of the most venomous strikers in Britain. Tall, husky, fearless, Parlane is adored by the Rangers' supporters.

He has made the boys in light blue forget about Colin Stein, that ever-running, ever-bustling Scotland centre-forward who was transferred to Coventry City, and played a big part in Rangers' success story last season.

His story is one of the strange romances of Scottish football, a story which illustrates all the disappointment, drama and

had gone crazy. The trend was set in England. With money no object, the market became a merry-go-round. Fans wondered from week to week which of their stars would go—and who would join their club. It was, as the warning bells sounded disaster for football all over the country, a sad commentary that the only solution was to buy and sell, buy and sell, buy and sell.

Scotland was hit, of course. We usually are, though the big stories were being written in England. Take this example

All the enthusiasm, fearlessness and mobility of Derek Parlane is shown in the Rangers' striker's all out bid to foil the Airdrie defence.

spectacular success which are never far away from each other in our national game.

Not so long ago, the fans would have laughed at the thought of Parlane, son of a former senior player, ever being a striker. He was just one of a host of other youngsters on the Ibrox staff, not bad, not great, but promising—not as a forward but as a midfield player.

Life changed for Derek, however, when the elegant Davie Smith broke a leg. Manager Jock Wallace decided Smith needed special treatment to give him confidence in his battle to regain fitness.

That's when Parlane was called in. The manager instructed the two players to get together at the Ibrox practice ground. Dave was told: 'Take the ball to Derek and try to dribble past him.' Derek was ordered: 'Try your best to take the ball from Davie and give him a tough time.'

The unusual treatment worked. Smith soon forgot his leg had been broken. And, at the same time, Parlane learned to use his height and weight.

And Wallace thought to himself: 'The way that boy Parlane sets about his work he may be a better striker than he would ever be in the middle.'

Parlane quickly got the chance to show he could be the new Colin Stein. One Sunday morning, the Rangers youth team were about to depart for Amsterdam and a tournament. At a special training session, Derek Parlane impressed his boss at shooting practice.

'When I saw just how hard Derek could thump that ball, I made up my mind finally that he just had to be a striker,' said Wallace.

The experiment began. Derek was tried out as striker in a third team game against East Stirling.

Now international honours beckon. Derek realises he still has a long way to go before he really reaches the top. But his progress has been sensational.

He was the find of the season.

One of the reasons for his rise to fame has been his enthusiasm. But you can be sure Derek is curbing his feelings. He was the first Scottish player to have his name taken for running off the field after scoring —against Ayr United in the Scottish Cup semi-final at Hampden—and saluting the fans.

Referees had been instructed to curb this—and Derek paid the penalty.

Is Sir George right? Or...

Can two cheeky chappies help Scotland win the World Cup?

MANY people in Scotland agreed with Sir George Graham, that greatly respected legislator who was with the Scottish Football Association from 1929 until 1957, when, forthright as always even at the age of 80, he said bluntly in an interview: 'Scotland have no chance of winning the World Cup.'

Now retired as secretary of the SFA, Sir George pulled no punches when asked about our chances of winning the premier tournament to be held in Munich in 1974. Said Sir George: 'We will never win the World Cup because we are just not good enough, we don't have the basic skills and we run at the game too hard.

'We don't need a team manager and I feel the numbers racket has ruined football. The game has changed and there's no fun about it. We're as far off winning the World Cup as I am off my first dinner.'

Sir George never sat on the fence. His views may be too frank for some—but they must be considered, for the former SFA secretary was one of our most distinguished legislators and authorities on the game.

Certainly it has been a long time since the Hampden Roar, football's most famous sound, as loud as a Wagnerian chorus, as fierce as the howl of a wolf pack, and as intimidating as the pounding of a cavalry charge, rocked our fortress of a stadium—on a really big game, that is, not on the minor international occasions—and it has

usually been a whisper on World Cup occasions.

Our World Cup story is a lament, a carbon copy of Scotland's history, which contains more disasters like Flodden, the Darien Scheme, and Glencoe than victories like Bannockburn.

Sir George's remarks merely rubbed salt into the wounds of a dreadful World Cup history....

Failure to qualify in 1950 because Willie Bauld of Hearts hit the bar against England and we didn't go to South America because we didn't win the home international series ... tragedy in Switzerland in 1954, when, after a worrying time, we were humiliated by Uruguay ... shocking team selection in Sweden in 1958, when we really had a chance, that cost us victory in the crucial game against Paraguay ... touches of bad luck, admittedly, in 1962 when we just failed to qualify ... and sorrowful stories of abject defeat in 1966 and 1970.

This time we made a better start by beating Denmark (but I'm afraid that as this has to be written before the other crucial games the results of our clashes with the tough Czechs aren't known).

Even then, the fans could hardly disagree with Sir George, for they feel cynical about reports that Scotland is once again on the verge of a new era. To them 'new era' is a dirty phrase, an old, tired cry that

28

rises every time we seem to be achieving success, then dies to a whisper when our team fails to follow through. We've been having 'new eras' since the days Alex James's pants flapped round his knees—and none of them have lasted longer than the stamina of a player out on the booze the night before a big match.

And the events of last season on the international front brought back that old yo-yo sensation to me.

So sudden are the changes that a reporter's viewpoint changes like the wind.

For instance, just before we beat Denmark at Hampden I had the feeling that times had changed, that Scotland was at last on the edge of something vitally important.

Scotland, who had failed so often against the Cinderella countries, had played against Denmark almost ruthlessly, combining the artistry of yesterday with the solid method of the 1970s.

I thought we were on the way back. In Tommy Docherty, as optimistic as Sir George Graham is pessimistic, we had an ebullient, enthusiastic manager who knows the modern game, understands players, and has the technical ability to plan a match in 1972.

We had also rid ourselves of what I believe is the real reason for failure in the past. Not foolishness on the field, undermining by the top brass, or failure by clubs to give this country the players she needed. No, perhaps the real reason for our tragic World Cup campaigns has been a 'too guid a conceit of ourselves' complex. Even today there are Scots who think, like the Stuarts, we have a divine right—a divine right in our case to the greatest players in the world, a divine right to be masters of the soccer globe.

Which, of course, is rubbish. We're a small country. We do produce fine players.

Derek Johnstone of Rangers can help Scotland to World Cup success. Here he is in attack—but it is at centre-half that he is making a great name for himself.

But so do other nations. And others, without our silly pride and prejudice, gear the great ability of their stars to a stern method and unchallenged organisation.

Docherty saw the light. He had a plan, stuck to it, didn't chop and change for changing's sake. Scotland had become a good, modern team who could pace an international. We seemed to have got over an old failing and found players who could hit the back of the net.

I was impressed with Docherty's instructions in Denmark. He fused the new with the old. 'We must have hitters,' he said. Those who thought he was turning to the physical were reassured when he described the ball driven hard into the packed goal area as the most difficult to deal with. He said the mid-field men would be hitters and the wingers would be hitters, and when they drove the ball hard it would break off defenders or disturb or hurt them and that the nippy men in the middle would live off the crumbs. Peter Lorimer of Leeds was to be hitter-in-chief.

And it worked—brilliantly.

'We must be bright on the wings,' Docherty said. Not the old type of wingers, however, who danced down the touchline and sent over high crosses. But wingers in the new tradition—with Lorimer providing the power and the audacity and the big shot. With Willie Morgan of Manchester United providing the boundless energy and running power in mid-field, then breaking down the left line.

Added the Doc: 'Our aim is to get goals. I feel the ultra-sophisticated football era is over. I combine method with art.'

So we had two good results against Denmark. The Doc was right. The team was right. The drill was right, the spirit right.

That's what I was writing in the winter of 1972.

Now . . . well, I'm back to the old days,

to what I have been writing, alas, for so long: 'Having reported more World Cup campaigns than most, I am hardly naive, unlikely to be fooled by a couple of results, and I have too often in the past toasted success, only to drink bitter dregs a short time later.

For what happened?

Docherty left Scotland to become manager of Manchester United. Lorimer was ordered off against Denmark at Hampden —and so we can't have our hitter-in-chief for the key games against Czechoslovakia.

The old, sad Scottish lament again.

Nevertheless, while it is distressing that we have once again to chop and change in the middle of a World Cup campaign, I am not as pessimistic as my old friend, Sir George.

There's a new man in charge—World Cup Willie. He's Willie Ormond, former manager of St. Johnstone and a talented winger with Hibernian when they were the wonder of all the soccer world.

Unlike Docherty, he is no extrovert. But he also likes to combine the confections of yesteryear with the steel core of today.

His start was not the best. But Ormond knows what he wants. Like Docherty, he saw the perfect example of how not to run a World Cup team, for he and the Doc played together in the shambles of 1954, when incredible blunders put Scotland out of her first World Cup in Switzerland.

Scotland had sent only 13 players to Switzerland—and two of them were goalkeepers.

Some feel Ormond may be too audacious, too imaginative. He likes football adventure, loves attacking, entertaining play, which seems to be a fault in these sombre soccer days. . . .

But Willie will learn. He has always been an ambitious student of the game,

Going into a tackle is the elegant George Connelly, of Celtic—one of the two cheeky chappies who can make Scotland great again.

with stints as player, coach, trainer and manager.

And, like Docherty, he will realise that there must be stern method as well as artistry in a modern World Cup team.

Anyhow, Ormond is well up in modern thinking. He went to the German coaching school in Munich not so long ago with Docherty and Hibs manager Eddie Turnbull.

He says: 'I go a long way with Tommy Docherty. He likes attackers getting round opposing defences wide and he likes to have strength in the right places. Like him, too, my thinking involves attack, perhaps because of my background. I played with great attackers and was conditioned by them. I can play defensively if that is needed, but I am happier when going forward.'

If he has a weakness, it is that he doesn't like too many men in the middle. Docherty did—and flourished. So far Ormond's tactics have been praiseworthy, but hardly overflowing with success.

Yet there's plenty going for Ormond and Scotland. We can have the elegant impertinence of Baxter in the composed play of these two newcomers, George Connelly of Celtic and Derek Johnstone of Rangers.

Can a new Scotland be built round these two cheeky chappies?

Some feel they're too clever, too imaginative, not dourly strong enough in a modern defence.

I'm not so sure. We need method, sure —but no *great* Scottish team can ever succeed by robot-like play.

As I keep preaching, it's the men of culture, of extra class who make teams magnificent.

Perhaps Connelly and Johnstone, with the right, tough, hard men around them, can put Willie Ormond on the map—and confound Sir George Graham, who, I know, would be happier than most to see his beloved country take the top football honour.

But we have to wait—and hope.

Power—that's what Peter Lorimer of Leeds has got. Here the sharpshooting Peter, who will be missed against Czechoslovakia, nets in an international against Ireland.

Centenary Pageant

It's the 100 up for the SFA, Rangers and Hearts

All the excitement of a century of soccer

For Scottish football, 1973 is a red-letter year.

It's the year the Scottish Football Association, Rangers and Hearts all celebrate their centenary.

For 100 years, then, our soccer has been organised on a national basis. For 100 years, Scottish football has been growing up. For 100 years, sweeping changes have been turning a primitive, often savage sport into the sophisticated, streamlined game which is now the most popular in the world.

Scotland played a major part in the sport's development. We can be proud of our achievements, happy that the SFA, Rangers and Hearts have contributed in no small measure to a century of swinging soccer.

As always, the part played by Queen's Park, the pioneers, can never be forgotten. Nor can we forget, either, that in 1973 as in 1873 what the supporter relishes most is 'a real guid gemme'.

Let's look back over the years, recalling the great events, the significant changes of a century, and trace the glittering pageantry of Scottish football's first 100 years.

This is the Scottish Football Book's tribute to the SFA, Rangers and Hearts.

May your next 100 years in football be just as happy and significant as your first 100—not out!

SFA — How it all started

I T wasn't drink the boys in the backroom of the little Glasgow hotel in Bridge Street were demanding on the cold night of 13 March 1873.

After all, it was a temperance establishment and there was serious business afoot for the long-whiskered men of the eight football clubs who were present.

What the backroom boys sought was the start of a bright new era for Scottish soccer —and on that historic night 100 years ago the resolute pioneers formed the Scottish Football Association.

The original members were Queen's Park, Clydesdale, Dumbreck, Vale of Leven, Eastern, 3rd LRV, Rovers and

Granville. They were later in the year joined by Alexandra Athletic, Southern, Callander Blythswood, Western, Renton, Dumbarton and Kilmarnock.

But the SFA was the brainchild of Queen's Park. Why not? In those far off days, Queen's Park *were* Scottish football,

A notable picture from the past—all the way from Canada. It shows a Kilmarnock team —and opponents—who went on tour in North America as far back as 1930, the year after the Ayrshire club had won the Scottish Cup.

having been founded in 1867. The Hampden amateurs joined the Football Associa-

tion of England, the only governing body then in existence, in November, 1870.

No other Scottish clubs, however, were willing to go in with Queen's, which was hardly surprising—for where could they obtain the money to travel frequently to England?

Queen's Park, though, achieved epic deeds. They proudly carried Scotland's banner high in the English Cup, then assumed the great responsibility of playing the first international against England in 1872, providing all the Scottish players and holding the Sassenach to a 0–0 draw.

But Queen's felt a club against a country wasn't fair odds—and even then there was keen rivalry between Scotland and England.

Anger, too. Because the English FA had begun internationals between their country and Scotland—and had picked BOTH teams. Although the Scots fumed, there seemed little they could do about it—for there was no ruling authority in the country.

The Scotland teams—picked by the English — played four pseudo internationals, losing three and drawing one, from 1870 to 1872. All the Scots were resident south of the border—no doubt the start of that well-known animosity often displayed against Anglos in more modern times.

So Queen's challenged the presumptuous English to a real international and this audacious adventure of club against country started the Scottish club thinking it was high time our country, too, had a national association.

Also, Queen's Park felt a cup competition was essential if soccer were to become popular in Scotland. Certainly the English FA tournament started in 1871–72 had proved a big hit and so, on 8 February 1873, Queen's Park secretary Archibald Rae wrote to other Scottish clubs proposing 'a Scotch Cup for competition among Scotch clubs next season'.

At the meeting in March the representatives of the eight clubs agreed to promote the Scotch Cup, later the Scottish Football Challenge Cup, and to form themselves into the Scottish Football Association. The first secretary was, naturally, Archibald Rae of Queen's Park.

So the start of the SFA was modest. But it was effective. The credit balance at the end of the first year was £1 11s. 4d.—and the Scottish Cup was firmly established.

The clubs subscribed for a trophy which, with 12 silver medals for the winners, cost £56 12s. 11d.

When you realise the enormous amounts this old cup of ours has raised, you can say it has certainly paid its way. And so the SFA began to make football the world's most popular sport. More and more clubs joined—Rangers, Barrhead, 3rd Edinburgh, Arthurlie, Thistle, Clyde, Celtic, Hearts, St. Mirren, Hibs, and all the others we know today.

These were carefree soccer days, the days of wine and gaiety, of 'smoke and pewter'—as historians described the happy parties held after every match.

Football was a sport, not a business. You could buy a ball in the 1880's, for instance, for less than 10s. A Glasgow emporium sold jerseys at 4s. 6d. and cowls, an essential part of the equipment even if it had players resembling pirates, at 1s. Boots were 8s. 6d. a pair.

Some of the rules were: No. 3—After a goal is won, ends shall be changed . . . 4—A goal shall be won when the ball passes between the goal-posts under the tape . . . 10—No player shall wear any nails nor iron plates or gutta percha on the soles or heels of his boots.

Football quickly grew up, though, and the SFA had many complex problems to deal with. There was the rise of professionalism, made legal by the SFA in 1893. There were rows with England over rules and laws of the game. There were internationals to organise, even one against Canada in 1891. There were tours to organise and pioneer coaches to be sent abroad to spread the allure of soccer.

There was also the problem of a home for the SFA. For four years the association remained in the humble place of its birth in Bridge Street, at a cost of 3s. a night. Then offices were rented in succession at

36

Something, alas, we don't see nowadays. Action during an Ireland-Scotland match at Windsor Park, Belfast. But because of the trouble over the water Scotland don't play in Northern Ireland any more.

Dundas Street, Carlton Place and Waterloo Street.

Just before the turn of the century, however, the SFA were in residence again in Carlton Place, a house once the home of a Glasgow merchant prince. Now they look down over the city of Glasgow from their imposing building high in Park Gardens.

Today the SFA are still highly regarded in the world of football. They can look back with pride on their 100 years of achievement. They have kept football alive in this country, despite constant criticism.

The next 100 years may be even more worrying than the first century of Scottish soccer—but the lessons of the past have been learned and victories in battles which were momentous at the time will keep this country in the forefront of football legislation.

The first match under lights

IN a century of football organised by the SFA, there have been many events whose magnitude was not realised at the time.

And to my mind nothing has been more important in the past 100 years than the introduction of floodlight football.

Soccer by night allows us to stage glamorous games during the week which can be watched by thousands without having to take time off work.

Can you imagine what the game might have been like today if it hadn't been for those pylons and flaring lights which are as much part of the modern soccer scene as a high flat is of living in a city?

There might never have been torrid European competitions . . . nearly all big games might have had to be played on a Saturday afternoon . . . football would never have developed as glamorously as it has without the excitement generated by artificial lighting.

Yet soccer by floodlight has really only come into vogue in the past 20 years.

So it may surprise you to know that a Scottish club organised a match on a winter's night . . . 95 years ago.

In the 1870's, just as organised football was getting into its swing, a serious problem was that of getting the players together on a Saturday afternoon in time to finish a match before darkness set in.

Working hours were longer on Saturdays then, for one thing. For another, players, mostly men of substance, were a convivial lot and it wasn't unknown for a refreshment or two to be quaffed as they met in a hostelry before a game. And the licensing laws in those days did not demand that customers left sharply on the stroke of 2.30 pm.

Football mind turned to the problem of playing matches by night and Kilmarnock F.C. became the pioneers in the floodlight business, organising the first 'great match played with electric light in Ayrshire'—to quote an old Killie historian.

The date of the first floodlight game to be played in Scotland was Friday night, 8 November 1878. 'An immense number

A great Scot of not so long ago, Dave Mackay, of Spurs, lining up in a match against Celtic.

One of the greatest of all
back-room teams in a century
of soccer—Celtic's Neil
Mochan, Jock Stein, Sean
Fallon and Bob Rooney.

of people assembled at Rugby Park to see the novel game between Kilmarnock and Kilmarnock Portland' and there were three lights, power for which was provided by a traction engine.

In 1893, Celtic also experimented with football under the lights. They asked near neighbours Clyde to play a friendly by night.

A crowd of around 5,000 turned up and the field was illuminated by 16 arc lamps, hung from high poles erected inside the track with a row suspended up the middle of the field.

But the evening of Christmas Day, 1893, was foggy and proved unfavourable to the experiment.

The match ended in a 1–1 draw but didn't prove as exciting as anticipated—perhaps because the players were instructed to keep the ball on the ground so that the lights strung across the ground would not be hit by high clearances.

But the shadows were dangerous and the electric light of that period was inclined to flicker.

The experiments did not continue, one other reason being that the machinery proved far too costly for the amateur clubs of the period to bear.

Nevertheless, can you imagine football today without floodlighting?

And can you imagine football without the Scottish League?

But there was heartburning, especially at Hampden, when the idea of a league was mooted in the late 1880's.

Even better organisation than that provided by the SFA was felt to be necessary. Except in the cups, the games were merely 'club matches'—and, of course, every club wanted to play against what they considered to be the best of the others. This caused discontent.

In 1888, an organisation had been formed in England under the title of the Football League, whose function was to regulate the playing of a series of matches which would at the same time provide competitive interest.

The proposal to form a Scottish League, though, was looked on as the forerunner of the introduction of professionalism and a diehard section, led by Queen's Park, was ready to fight to the bitter end. However, in 1890, the League started—and it has been justified since our game would never have prospered if a keen competition set-up had been ignored.

Money was beginning to talk in soccer

39

—and now our big clubs in the League constitute to most what football is about.

Incidentally, in all the talk of reconstruction, let it be recalled that at one time there were three divisions—just after the First World War, that was.

The Third Division was not a success, however, and was discontinued in favour of two divisions, then with 20 and 18 clubs in the First and Second respectively.

Today the SFA and the League live in harmony—and let it be remembered that the SFA look after EVERYONE in soccer, not only the top clubs.

No-one is more passionate about football than the Scot. A defeat is invariably a disaster, a victory an epic triumph. We exaggerate with all the woe and wonder of a bard.

And in 100 years of football history, we feel there is nothing more lamentable than our failures in the World Cup—and nothing more heroic than the success of the Wembley Wizards in 1928.

There's a link.

For some people believe that it was the fault of the Wizards, who beat England 5–1 at Wembley, that Scotland have such a sorry record in the World Cup.

They allege that because of the Wizards we refuse to look to the present—and will succeed in global modern soccer only when we forget about the Wizards, class them as a missile expert would bowmen at Flodden and choose Scotland elevens in the 1970's manner—with the accent on drill, drill, drill—and power.

Too many experts, say the critics, still —as perhaps Manchester United did— put their faith in the free expression of the Wizards, as out of date nowadays as Alex James's famous down-to-the-knees pants.

You can argue all day. I still maintain that the Wizards gave Scotland her most

Will there ever be a Scotland or Rangers' skipper as great as George Young?

joyous day in football—for there is no doubt that they were the best collection of GOOD footballers we ever assembled.

And the Scots' glorious passing moves, triangular tangos that had the frantic English going the wrong way, will always be one of soccer's most magnificent purple patches. Scotland that day of 1928 played football as cultured and as beautiful as any seen at any time, any place.

There have been alas, many dark days as well as afternoons of sweet delight in the history of Scottish soccer. The game always arouses passions—and one of the worst outbreaks was at Hampden in 1909.

A battle raged on the pitch. Flames crackled and smoke billowed skyward from burning pay-boxes. Stones were hurled at ambulance men racing to aid the many casualties.

And this riot broke out because of a silly misunderstanding. The crowd at the

What the well-dressed footballers of 40 years ago were wearing. McPhail, Scotland, and Blenkinsop, England, shake hands before the start of a 1934 international.

Wingers have always played a great part in the history of Scottish football. Here are two of the greatest—Willie Henderson, Rangers, and Jimmy Johnstone, Celtic.

Rangers–Celtic Cup Final replay of 17 April, 1909, had expected extra time—and they stormed the ground when they didn't get it.

A newspaper had misled the fans by stating that, in the event of a draw, there would be an extra half-hour. But at that time the Cup rules did not permit extra time.

Thousands joined the hotheads who had started the trouble by demanding what they called 'their rights'. For nearly two hours a battle raged. Barricading was torn

down—and made into a huge bonfire, set alight with oil stolen from a nearby store. When the fire brigade arrived, the howling mob assaulted the firemen and cut their hoses.

An atom bomb would have caused little more damage to the ground and immediate neighbourhood—and it took several days to dig out all the broken glass embedded in the ground.

We Scots are also inclined to become irate when we read of yet another of our soccer stars going south at a huge fee. But

42

our indignation now is nothing to that aroused in the old days.

In the 1880's, indeed, a war almost broke out between Scotland and our neighbours south of the border, so bitter was the animosity aroused by the start of professionalism.

How did professionalism start?

Mainly, I fancy, because England became jealous of Scotland's skill at soccer. And 'veiled professionalism' crept in when English clubs realised they were greatly inferior to the Scots. So enter the new border raiders of the 1880's.

In an effort to copy Scottish soccer style, English clubs lured northern experts south— 'for a consideration'. Payment, of course, was still highly illegal.

The SFA tried to take action—for Scotland was being drained of her best players. They were helped by the FA. But still the Scots crowded every team in Lancashire, where prosperous mill-owners wanted to boost their prestige by directing great football teams . . . and were willing to pay loads o' brass to players on the side.

In July 1885, the SFA felt they were stabbed in the back by the English—for that was when the FA officially recognised professionalism.

The SFA decided to fight. Our clubs, who could not afford to pay wages, were losing their best players. All SFA clubs were forbidden to play against professionals. The football war between Scotland and England became bitter. The SFA refused even to allow Dr John Smith, a Queen's Park player, to assist the Corinthians, a band of the whitest simon pures, in the annual New Year's match in 1889 at Hampden. And Scotland made it clear they would not play the annual international with England if professionals were to be included.

Professionals were hunted and harried.

Scottish soccer was rich in characters—and here's one of the greatest. It's Jim Baxter, of Rangers, tossing the trophy in the air after a great cup victory.

Two cases of professionalism were proved in Scotland, the players suspended for two years and a club, Hearts, expelled from the SFA for a month.

A list was drawn up of players who had crossed the border to play for money. There were 68 names on it—and they were all banned from playing in Scotland.

But the march of progress couldn't be stopped. Scottish clubs realised that professional teams in England were the best in the world and demanded that professionalism be allowed here.

In 1893 Celtic brought the matter up once again at the annual meeting of the SFA—and they won the case for the paid player.

The first super league in 1891

As the SFA celebrate their centenary this year, it might pay them to look back into their glorious past—and find solutions to problems which will arise in the next 100 years.

Buried in the millions of words which have been written about soccer since the SFA were formed in 1873 are stories which would seem new if written today—stories of deeds and events which could create modern sensations.

For instance, there was a super league —away back in 1891. Not just an ordinary league. But the type of league so many people imagine would bring new prosperity to football in these trying times of the 1970's—a Scottish-English competition.

It began because Queen's Park refused to join the Scottish League. They were opposed to professionalism.

Denis Law was one of the all-time great Scotland attackers. Not everyone's favourite, of course—but what exciting football he gave us when he was on form. No-one could score goals like Denis. He deserves an honoured place in Scotland's centenary parade.

But trouble loomed for the Queen's, still a power in the land. Once they could have their pick of opponents. Now, with the Scottish League formed, they discovered teams like Rangers, Third Lanark, Vale of Leven and Dumbarton, then also among the powerful elite, would not give them a fixture because of their new commitments.

Once again, however, the noted Queen's Park fighting spirit flared. They got down to work—and what a treat there was in store for Scottish fans.

Matches were arranged with Everton, Corinthians, Canadians, Notts Forest, Sunderland the Preston North End as well as with home clubs not yet in the league—Kilmarnock, Battlefield, St Bernard's, Hamilton Acas, Leith Athletic, Falkirk, Thistle, Northern and Airdrie.

Aye, that was in 1889—and the pick of Scotland and England engaged in super soccer clashes.

The idea was attractive—just as visionaries say it would be today. Anyhow, Queen's prospered. They made a great profit out of this super league—£3,201, tremendous indeed for that day and age. And they had no professionals to pay.

Another feature of the past which, according to the cynical, might be revived is—an umpire for both teams!

That was the rule at the start of the SFA's reign. Then came a neutral umpire who could give a decision only if appealed to. Now we have the referee and neutral linesmen.

But what drama there would be if again we had the breath-taking spectacle of the two umpires holding a conference to decide the correct decision—and maybe punching each other on the nose!

What's new in football? The special train? Not at all. In the Cup Final of 1881 between Queen's Park and Dumbarton

played at Rangers' ground at Kinning Park, Glasgow, the Boghead fans were conveyed by a soccer special. And not one seat was ripped.

All-ticket games? Well, in 1884, Third Lanark offered Cathkin to the SFA for all their matches, including the Scotland v England international. The SFA accepted. And inside a few days the jolly old Thirds had tickets on issue at 5s each. They called them 'seasons'—and the SFA joined in and issued tickets at 3s for the international.

Who, though, can say what football will be like in the next 100 years. Gates are still falling, it's true. But the game is still the most popular in the world. It won't die, that's for sure.

I feel soccer will be streamlined in the future—and the next 100 years must see the demise of small clubs in waters that are too deep for them.

This will surely be the gravest issue for the SFA, whose concern is football at all levels, in the near future. They must form

We've always been proud of our great Scottish inside-forwards and here's a master of his craft who will never be forgotten, Jimmy Mason, of Third Lanark and Scotland.

new strata of soccer society. In the end, the masses will go only to the great games, to watch the great clubs.

In a way, it's a pity—for perhaps the happiest chapters in the long life of the SFA have been the epic feats of the little clubs throughout our soccer history.

For the pattern of Scottish soccer at the top hasn't been complex. It resolved itself simply into the Queen's Park era, then the Rangers–Celtic era, then the Rangers era, now the Celtic era, with neutral hopes that Edinburgh and Aberdeen might break it up.

Now and again, however, a wee club breaks through. And how we have relished the heroics of Vale of Leven, East Fife, Motherwell, Kilmarnock, Hearts, Hibs, Dundee and the few others who upset the three mighty giants (and Queen's Park are now out of it despite their magnificent start last century) who hold the monopoly of Scottish honours.

There's no thrill like an Old Firm thrill. Rival skippers John Greig and Billy McNeill shake hands—something we've seen almost since the dawn of soccer history, something we know will provide football's most blazing excitement—a Rangers-Celtic clash.

My wish for the next epoch in Scotland is—the appearance of another Renton. They will always be my favourite club.

For they became the first champions of the world, this little village team who trained on 'Chicken Bree'. They won the Scottish Cup in 1887—then challenged West Bromwich Albion, who had taken the English Cup. They beat them, too— and declared themselves world title holders in the soccer world.

Renton's fine win over the English cup-holders was the more significant in that West Brom had boasted that their victory in the cup was the first by an all-English team.

One of the best of all Scottish goalkeepers—Ronnie Simpson of Celtic.

When they first followed Rangers

WHEN Rangers celebrated their centenary with a fabulous match against Ajax of Holland, the club champions of the world, on 16 January 1973, their record was imposing—34 Scottish League championships, 19 Scottish Cup victories, 37 Glasgow Cup wins, 32 Charity Cup successes and seven League Cup triumphs.

They had also won the European Cup-winners Cup in 1972 and they have given to Scotland international elevens far more players than any other club in the country.

Yet it is ironic to think that the club might never have become world famous if in 1873 a young man hadn't picked up a football and spoken the words familiar to every schoolboy: "If I don't get a game, you can't play with my ball".

Early in 1873 there were no Rangers. Of the handful of clubs in existence, Queen's Park alone had won renown and there would have been raucous laughs from Hampden if Queen's had been told that a few lads, mostly from the Gareloch who had come to the city of Glasgow to find fame and fortune, were about to start a football club which would become even mightier and more successful than Queen's Park.

The Gareloch boys were really more interested in a pastime which evoked memories of their lochs of home—rowing. But as they hauled their boats ashore on the upper reaches of the Clyde at Glasgow Green one afternoon they watched the players of the Eastern Football Club prac-

48

One of the greatest players of all time—Rangers' wee blue devil, Alan Morton.

tising on a piece of ground known as the Fleshers Haugh.

They joined in, soon forgot about rowing and talked about forming a football club of their own. But it was merely talk. Until, that is, one of the lads, William McNeill, was gifted a football.

The others proposed that a club be formed with this ball as a starting point. They also said that William McNeill was too old to be admitted to membership. At that, the huffed William picked up the ball and said: 'If I don't get a game, you don't play with my ball'.

This merely strengthened the determination of the others to go ahead. They held a meeting and started a subscription to buy a ball. When he realised his friends meant business, William changed his mind and, with his brothers Harry, Moses and Peter, became one of the stalwarts of the early Rangers team. It was undoubtedly his refusal to allow the others to play with his ball, however, that really led to the formation of Rangers.

The Gareloch lads had the ball. They also had the use of a piece of ground at Fleshers Haugh. The next business was: What to call the new club? At first, they fancied the name, Argyle.

And today the legions of fans might be singing, 'There's not a team like the Glasgow Argyle' if Moses McNeill hadn't been given a copy of an English football annual for that year. He was attracted by the name of an English Rugby club. It was: The Rangers. The name appealed to the rest of the gang and they adopted it as their own. So Rangers, now so typically Scottish, nevertheless owe something to England.

Enthusiasm for Rangers mounted as the Gareloch boys became more accomplished in the arts and crafts of this new game, football.

Soon they bought complete strips, scrimping on food to find the money. There was little argument about the colours. Royal blue shirts, white knickers and blue and white stockings—that was the popular choice.

Incidentally, in 1879, Rangers thought a change of colours would bring greater success so they switched to shirts with blue and white hoops. Their fortunes had declined and their secretary, Mr Angus Campbell, a true Highlander not above superstition, decided luck would change if they had a new strip. It didn't. Rangers reverted to their old royal blue in 1883.

It was high summer when Rangers set out on the football adventures which were to take them to the peak of success. As Rangers improved, they wanted to play the more formidable teams. Then, as now, nothing but the best would do for Rangers.

At that time the Big Four were Queen's Park, Vale of Leven, Third Lanark and Clydesdale and at first they were snooty, feeling it was below their dignity to play the boys of Glasgow Green. At last, however, Vale of Leven condescended to give Rangers a match. The result was sensational. Rangers drew with the mighty Vale.

Then they played in the Scottish Cup of 1874–5 and beat Oxford on the Queen's Park Recreation Ground, losing in the next round, however, to Dumbarton.

Soon Rangers secured a ground of their own. They swithered about building at Shawfield, then decided a pitch at Burnbank, near Glasgow's Great Western Road, suited them better and they occupied it for season 1875–76.

It was during their stay at Burnbank that Rangers were involved in an amazing incident. They beat 3rd LVR (Third Lanark) in a second round Scottish Cup-tie. But Third protested—and succeeded. But even junior clubs who employ MI5 methods to find a reason for a replay wouldn't have the temerity to go as far as the 3rd LVR did. Their complaint was that during the tie Rangers had once kicked off when their opponents should have done so. The SFA, however, sustained the protest and 3rd won the replay 2–0—and went on to lose to Queen's Park in the final.

Now that Rangers had secured their own enclosure, they realised their greatest ambition, for Queen's Park, then the No 1 club in football, could no longer persist in refusing to play them. It was a great game and though Rangers lost 2–0 they were not disgraced and they knew they were on the way up.

In 1876 they moved to Kinning Park, where they took over a lush green pitch, formerly the property of Clydesdale. It was fitting that in the season Rangers occupied their fine new ground they should figure in their first Scottish Cup Final. It was against the redoubtable Vale of Leven, who had just earned undying football fame, having qualified to meet Rangers in the final by becoming the first Scottish team ever to defeat Queen's Park.

Rangers' first cup final was played at Hamilton Crescent in Glasgow. And the young team shocked Vale by holding them to a 0–0 draw. An even bigger crowd attended the replay, also at Hamilton Crescent. Again Rangers rose to the big occasion and at the end of the game, with the score 1–1, the teams agreed to play an extra half hour.

Remember, there were no goal nets in those days, nor crossbars. So, with only a few minutes left to play of the extra 30 minutes, Peter Campbell of Rangers shot fiercely. "Goal" bellowed the jubilant

Rangers supporters. But in a second the cheers were stilled. Vale goalkeeper Wood had the ball in his hands and was kicking it away. Play stopped.

Rangers claimed the ball had passed through the goal. Vale men said it hadn't. Spectators joined in the row. They invaded the field. Pandemonium. The game ended abruptly and a replay was ordered.

The third match was played at Hampden Park and this time Vale of Leven won 3–2.

This was the start of Rangers' amazing ill-fortune in the Scottish Cup. At certain periods in their history the Ibrox team have been dogged by a cup jinx.

Today they are Rangers the mighty, Rangers the magnificent. But they had their crises in the early days. In their first 20 years, for instance, Rangers had only one real triumph, when they won the Glasgow Charity Cup in 1878–9.

And they ran into trouble, mainly because some of their fine young players, in the phrase of the day, 'succumbed to the lure of the Saxon sovereign'.

With their stars going south—as so many Scots still do today—weakened Rangers started to slide. They lost game after game. Enthusiasm waned. In the early 1880s there was a financial crisis, which was solved only by their president, George Goudie, giving the club £30 out of his own pocket to keep Rangers going.

Rangers fought on, however, and they took part in the English Cup, as did other Scottish clubs in those days.

Indeed, they reached the semi-final in 1886 and lost to Aston Villa—mainly because goalkeeper Willie Chalmers had too big a lunch!

He was a noted trencherman and he met an old friend at lunch. So well did he do himself that he confessed ruefully after

Rangers had been beaten 3–1: 'I couldn't get about as quickly as usual.'

Rangers proudest day should have been 20 August 1887—for that was the date the first Ibrox Park was opened. The Ibrox district had been selected because their wise officials saw the spread westwards of Glasgow's teeming populace and the extension of the tram system in that direction.

Rangers determined to open the first Ibrox in style and a shrewd bargain—shrewdness being then, as now, one of the most striking points about Rangers' success—was made with Preston North End—shrewd because Preston, then known as the Invincibles were a great draw wherever they played and also because Preston agreed to play for £50 . . . while the drawings for the big game were to amount to £340.

The match, however, was anything but a cheerful christening for Ibrox. In a magnificent Preston team were great Scots like George Drummond, Sam Thomson, Dave Russell, Nick Ross and John Goodall.

Rangers were good but not great at that time—and at half-time they were five goals down. Then Preston added three more. The spectators, not so loyal then as they are now, decided they had seen enough. They howled for the match to be stopped. And it was.

But Rangers ploughed on grimly. They grew up. Big crowds were turning up to see the games. Rangers were on the threshold of fame. Soon professionalism was legalised in Scotland.

The first terms offered to Ibrox in 1893 were good—£5 a week in the first eleven and £1 in the reserves. That was tremendous money in those days. And those were the wages Rangers players were paid when they won the Scottish Cup for the first time in 1893-4. So pleased were the Rangers

You could describe Jimmy Millar as a player 'in the real Ibrox tradition'. Jimmy was always a great favourite with the Rangers' fans.

officials at the win—which was over Celtic—that they gave the players a bonus, £3 3s. each.

But other clubs didn't pay as well. Take the great Alec Smith. Before the famous player from Darvel was signed by Rangers, he was invited to join Kilmarnock, whose terms were then 12s. 6d. for a win, 10s. for a draw and 7s. 6d. if they lost. Then Sunderland offered him £2 a week, later advanced to £2 10s. Smith turned this down, for he had been told that the regular Sunderland players received £3 a week, with the captain getting 5s. extra.

Players were proud in those days. There was the case of John Bell, from Slamannan, who joined Rangers in 1895. He was the goalkeeper in a cup-tie against Hibernian. Rangers lost. Bell thought he was responsible for the defeat. He dressed himself without a word to anyone, walked out of Ibrox—and was never seen there again. He didn't even call to collect the pay that was due to him.

At that time Rangers had goalkeeper trouble. But when they did find the right man, what a prince he was. And thanks to him Rangers reached the heights—and were to keep their proud place on the pinnacle of football fame from that day to this.

The player who solved their problems was Matthew Dickie, who arrived from Renton in 1895. The advent of this superb keeper put Rangers on the way to some of their greatest triumphs for it is still said that the team of 1896–7 was the best Ibrox had ever seen, mainly because of its keeper plus its brilliance in combination.

Rangers were glorious then. They won the Scottish Cup for the first time in 1894. In 1897 they won the 'Three Cups'—Scottish, Glasgow and Charity—and in season 1898–9 they won every league match played. They played 18 matches,

the league then having 10 clubs, but their opponents were the cream of Scotland's talent. In these 18 matches, Rangers scored 79 goals and lost 18.

The wonder team was: Dickie, Nick Smith, Crawford, Gibson, Neil, Mitchell, Campbell, McPherson, Hamilton, Miller and Alec Smith—every one an international.

And that's how Rangers were born, how they emerged from the dark days of football, from an awkward squad on a piece of waste ground to the club with the greatest support in Scotland.

They were to face more crises. They were to have big disappointments.

But the legend was made.

With 100 years of glorious history behind them, Rangers were entitled to celebrate their centenary in 1973 with all the pomp and pageantry of one of the most glamorous clubs in the world of football.

Rangers' heroes of today—Dave Smith and Tommy McLean, players who put the accent on artistry.

Hearts—
the club with style

Controversy rages over the date of the formation of Heart of Midlothian. Some historians say it was December, 1873; others maintain the famous old club wasn't in existence until the following year.

From the archives of Queen's Park, the pioneers of soccer in Scotland, I have discovered evidence, however, that Hearts were a club even before December, 1873.

As always, it was Queen's Park who made the game popular in Edinburgh. On 27 December 1873, as the Hampden chronicler of the time says: 'Queen's Park took to Edinburgh two teams to take part in a game as a missionary effort to popularise football in the East.'

The game took place on the ground of the Royal High School F.P. at Bonnington. But though the teams consisted mainly of Queen's Park players, there were several Hearts men in one of the sides and Hearts' first captain, Tom Purdie, always insisted that Hearts had been going as a club, albeit in a crude form, for many months before the Queen's Park match. The Hampden records confirm this.

Anyhow, other clubs came into being, including the Third Edinburgh Rifle Volunteers and the Thistle, a club who had played a mixture of football and handball but had become converted by the 'missionary' work of Queen's Park. Then followed a club called White Star. Most games were played in the Meadows, a green stretch to the south of the city which was once the Burgh Loch.

Gradually Hearts became the leaders and, in the end, most of the players of the other clubs joined the top dogs, who decided they needed something more than the public parks of the Meadows in which to demonstrate their skill at the new game of Association football.

They moved to the new Edinburgh Football Association's ground at Powburn, then had a spell at Powderhall and, in 1881, opened Tynecastle, one of the finest grounds in the country.

If there is argument about the date of Hearts' formation, no-one can deny that the club have produced some of the greatest and most colourful players in the history of the game. Hearts have always been rich in personalities and style, and, on looking wistfully back down the years, one imagines they had a monopoly of sleek inside-forwards, men with the velvet touch, players who formed one of the most famous schools, the old masters of the illustrious craft of Scottish inside-forwards.

One regret I have in football is that I never saw Bobby Walker, the true father of the distinctively Scottish type of inside-forward play which the best of the rest of the world copied—and still play to this day, for I maintain that the shining stars, the Cruyffs and the Beckenbauers, reveal exactly the moves which were first dreamed up by Scots.

53

It was in 1896 that Hearts found Robert Walker, a right-winger from Dalry Primrose. He quickly blossomed into an inside-forward of tremendous skill and for long he stood unique in Scotland with his 29 international caps — a remarkable number when you consider such honours then were only in respect of matches played against the home countries.

How good was Bobby Walker? His football was once summarised by a rueful Jack Robertson, who played for Rangers and then for the London Caledonian, later to become Chelsea: 'You would think Robbie had eight feet. You go to tackle him where his feet were—but they're away when you get there.'

From then on, Hearts have been blessed with inside-forwards of the highest calibre, another Walker, Tommy, Jimmy Wardhaugh, Jimmy Murray, Alfie Conn among them.

But there was only one Bobby Walker, a legend in his own lifetime.

He came out of retirement in 1915 to play in a Belgian Relief match at Tynecastle, his last appearance on the field. His wing partner was the equally fabulous Billy Meredith, the Welsh wizard. Between them, on the one wing, they had 75 caps. Walker 29 and Meredith 46.

It is to Hearts' credit that they are renowned for the quality of their football. Some of their fans, who want only success, may not be happy about this. I'm not so sure they should be worried. Hearts, like Partick Thistle, have been unpredictable. They are still the gay deceivers of Scottish soccer, stumbling too often when triumph is close at hand.

They were often the lily-gilders, overdoing clever football, of which they have always been capable. But the neutrals love to watch Hearts.

Because Hearts bring glamour . . . yes,

Hearts may not be as classy as they once were—but just as popular with the Tynecastle fans as any of the heroes of the past is dapper striker Donald Ford.

even today . . . to a football scene that is too often drab.

And what wonderful exponents of the crafts of the game they have presented.

Few of us ever saw Bobby Walker. But still a sweet dream to thousands of Tyne-

54

Now he's the Tynecastle trainer. Not so long ago he was recognised as one of the most superb Hearts players of all time. Yes, it's John Cumming, the man who never knew the meaning of the word defeat.

A great day for two stars who have had Tynecastle connections. Skippers George Miller, then with Hearts, and Roy Barrie, then with Dunfermline Athletic, await the result of the toss in the 1968 Cup Final. Barry, now in England, was also a Hearts stalwart. He was the winning captain in the 1968 final, Athletic beating Hearts 3–1.

castle is the thought of the Terrible Trio, Alfie Conn, Willie Bauld and Jimmy Wardhaugh, not so long ago the most attractive spearhead in Europe.

They had infinite resource, vivid imagination and moves as entrancing as any in the Hungarian or Brazilian handbook of football style. On their play was stamped the velvet glove touch of the manager of the period, Tommy Walker.

They made goal-scoring seem easy, they bewildered defences with quicksilver passing and acute positioning. They had perfect understanding, a little team within a team and they made Hearts great in the early 1950's.

I once wrote of them, 'They are a trio of distinction, each in his own right a player in the £20,000 class. Together . . . well, Hearts' fans say all the money in the Bank of England couldn't buy them!' That was in 1956. I wonder what these three would be worth in 1973. . . .

Hearts, like every other club, have known black days—and some of their worst moments were experienced in the 1880's.

In 1884, the burning question of the day was—professionalism! Scotland was bitterly against paying money to footballers and had to look bitterly at a stream of her most talented players going to England to spread the gospel of the game —and receive Saxon gold for their efforts.

But still we refused to countenance professionalism.

SFA drops a bombshell

Then Hearts beat Dunfermline 11–1. Dunfermline alleged there were professional footballers in the Hearts ranks and the SFA officially took up the accusation. A meeting was fixed for 21 October 1884 —just as Hearts were advertising a grand football challenge match with Blackburn Rovers, holders of the English Cup, to take place at Tynecastle on 23 October.

Then the SFA dropped a bombshell. They suspended Hearts for a breach of the Association laws on professionalism and disqualified for two years the two Hearts players who had played so well—a full-back, Maxwell, and a forward, McNee.

Scotland received the decision with mixed feelings. Some considered the expulsion of Hearts was necessary for the 'purification' of soccer in Scotland. Others sympathised with Hearts who, after all, had been singled out when it was generally known they had lost players through other clubs taking away their stars.

It was soon obvious the problem had not been solved, only shelved and that the pundits would have to think again. Hearts' suspension, however, was raised in time for them to play Blackburn. The English team won 1–0.

In 1885, however, England legalised professionalism but Scotland did not take the plunge until 1893.

It was several years after their formation that Hearts began to wear their famous maroon strip.

In the early days, a uniform strip was not compulsory. In April 1869, Queen's Park adopted their 'guernsey' shirt and cap—at a cost of 6s. a man. For a long time afterwards, however, players wore colours on their right arms to distinguish the teams. Up to 1876 players wore stockings of different colours—instead of modern numbers.

The first Hearts strip consisted of thick sweaters and long trousers. But the colours were then red, white and blue. Maroon was the colour worn by St. Andrew, a club of clever young players with whom Hearts, when in low water, joined.

When the new colour of maroon was adopted by Hearts, some of the older players continued to wear their original jerseys, dyed maroon, through which the stripes were still easily seen.

What was the early play like? It was, according to the Hearts distinguished historian, Albert Mackie, 'slow-paced. Dribbling was more in evidence than passing. The forwards played in two lines, three in front and three backing up. Because of the scarcity of clubs, Hearts had to be content with between 13 and 16 matches in the season, except for games played within the club between captain's and vice-captain's teams.'

Equipment was scarce and a different player every week was delegated to carry goal-posts to places like Kirkcaldy and Dundee when Hearts played away matches.

Players also had to pay their own expenses and often Hearts and Dundee arranged to play half-way in Fife to save money.

Hearts bear a proud name, Heart of Midlothian.

And the club have always demanded that their players adopt a standard of football and of conduct in keeping with its grand sound.

Let's hope that in their next hundred years Hearts continue to play enchanting football—and to win even more honours.

They are always known as the club with style.

A Hearts star of tommorrow? He's Eric Carruthers, a lad hoping to go places.

Centenary Blues

BACK TO SQUARE ONE

IT was to have been the football birthday party of the century, the day Scotland celebrated 100 years of glorious history by trouncing the country we most dearly love to beat, the auld enemy, England.

Alas, it turned out to be the flop of the century—and, on the night of 14 February 1973, disconsolate Scots suddenly realised how far behind in world football we were.

Looking back, however, the disaster at ice-cold Hampden served us right.

First, how daft it was to try to stage a soccer gala on a black February night, with the pitch cleared of snow but still iron-hard and treacherous, with far too many spectators standing ankle deep in snow on the terracings, cold, unhappy and uncaring.

Soccer pageantry calls for sunshine and martial music at its brightest and gay colour and a brave display of flags—not, when you compare it with Wembley, an apology for the pre-match entertainment on a bitterly cold evening which was put on at Hampden on 14 February.

Second, far too many Scots believed England were down and out, lambs to be led to the slaughter, with Sir Alf Ramsey bowing the knee to a Scotland side the naïve believed to be nearing world class.

We had forgotten that although, at that time, Scotland had won 35 to England's 32 in the bitter series between the countries our recent record had been deplorable against the Sassenach, our last victory, indeed, being as far back as 1967 at Wembley.

Nevertheless, there was optimism in the chill air. New team manager Willie Ormond, who had taken over from Tommy Docherty when the hearty Doc joined faltering Manchester United, was confident. 'I feel we can win this one well,' he said before the game.

He had chosen a side of which Docherty approved—for it was composed entirely from the squad the former manager most fancied. Some experts felt Pat Stanton, of Hibs, and Peter McCloy, of Rangers, should have been included on current form and others wondered if it was a justifiable decision to field five players from Manchester United, a club struggling to avoid relegation from the English First Division. And Scottish Nationalists were displeased because only two home Scots were included.

To be fair, however, Ormond's team found favour with practically everyone . . . before the match.

A crowd of 48,029 turned up despite the wintry weather and saw the sides line up like this:

Scotland: Clark (Aberdeen), Forsyth

No wonder Willie Ormond was looking worried. He had just started his new career as Scotland's manager, after being a famous winger with Hibernian and successful chief of St Johnstone. And what happened? Willie saw his side hammered 5–0 by England. Back to square one, back to the drawing board . . .

(Manchester United), Donachie (Manchester City), Bremner (Leeds United—capt), Colquhoun (Sheffield United), Buchan (Manchester United), Lorimer (Leeds United), Dalglish (Celtic), Macari,

Graham, Morgan (all Manchester United).

England: Shilton (Leicester), Storey (Arsenal), Hughes (Liverpool), Bell (Manchester City), Madeley (Leeds United), Moore (West Ham United—capt), Ball (Arsenal), Channon (Southampton), Chivers (Tottenham), Clarke (Leeds), Peters (Tottenham).

Referee: Robert Wurtz (France).

There was no hint at the start of the humiliation to come. Scotland made a promising start on a hard pitch covered with a thin layer of white, playing the short-passing, attractive game which had seen them do well in Brazil in the summer.

Peter Lorimer, the man with the thunderbolt shot, drove fiercely over in the first minute and then buzzing Lou Macari shot past.

But to the discerning it was obvious the England defence were unworried, especially imperturbable skipper Bobby Moore, who had received a silver salver before the match in recognition of his 100th cap for England—and the usual recognition from the Hampden crowd: loud boos and unfair chants.

And in five minutes the nightmare started. It was an own goal which was to signal 15 tragic minutes which would shatter Scotland.

A ball which carried no danger hurtled across the Scotland goal in England's first raid. The unfortunate Peter Lorimer somehow got in the way, connected with the ball—and was appalled to see it fly past Bobby Clark for the opening goal.

The silence which greeted this was deafening. And worse was to come.

Willie Morgan was hurt and as he limped Hughes punted a long ball up the middle. Confusion in the Scottish defence. Chivers and Colquhoun went up for the ball. The Scot slipped, faltered. The towering Chivers didn't. He won the ball

60

and directed it to Alan Clarke, called the Sniffer. The Leeds man sniffed well. Although his shot wasn't strong, it beat Clark, his Scottish namesake, and as early as 14 minutes the Scots were two down.

A minute later it was all over when the Scottish defence were caught again. It seemed our lads hadn't watched television, which so often features the prodigious throw-in of Martin Chivers. Anyhow, a long shy by the Spurs man again showed up the defenders in blue in a dreadful light and Mike Channon, who was to become the man of the match with sprightly raiding, nipped in at the near post to chip the ball over the line.

What a disaster after a neat start.

The crowd didn't like it. They howled for Colin Stein to be brought on. They got their wish. Morgan retired and on came the bustling Colin, once a Ranger and now making an even greater name for himself with Coventry, in 17 minutes.

As the fans were cheering Stein, Alan Clarke ran through unchallenged. He should have scored but hit over. A breathtaking let-off for the demoralised Scots.

The defence were deplorable. Clark was naturally anxious and he was beaten by a Chivers header and breathed a silent prayer when the ball hit the post.

Scotland could easily have been five down inside half an hour.

It was all over. No team in the world could present England with three goals and hope to pierce their immaculate defence.

To their credit, Scotland fought bravely but they found Peter Shilton in brilliant form in goal. The game became bogged down, with England content to look for

No wonder Bobby Clark looks disconsolate. He has just lost a goal. And he looked like this more than once, alas, in the centenary match against England. That, though, is the life of a goalkeeper. He's the man who always takes most blame. We don't forget that Bobby Clark has also played magnificently for his country and for his club, Aberdeen.

a break and try to hold the Scottish attackers, which was hardly a formidable task. England were far ahead in class and opportunism and had taken their lead the easy way. Much bigger than Scotland, they were nevertheless happier on the sad surface and instead of embroidering their play as the blue-shirts did they simply lobbed long balls into the panicking Scottish defence and ran behind them to make things so difficult for Bobby Clark.

Scotland did most of the attacking, looked quite good, and had latecomers, asking the score being told it was 3–0, thinking the home side were ahead. They didn't know England were taking it quietly, well aware the game had been won and lost.

Any slim chance Scotland had of saving the match went early in the second half. For once Shilton couldn't hold a shot. No wonder. It was a thundering free-kick taken by Lorimer. The ball slithered out of his grip and in ran Stein to pop it into the net. There was a roar of rage from the Scots when the referee insisted Stein was offside and ruled out the goal.

Then the English gatecrashers at what was to have been a Scottish party really took the icing off our birthday cake when they scored again through Chivers in the 77th minute, because of a Colquhoun blunder, and in the 86th minute, when Bobby Clark was slow to sense danger when Alan Clarke shot from an angle.

The 5–0 defeat was Scotland's worst result at Hampden since 1888, when we lost by the same score, and the fans left as stricken as Flodden camp followers.

So there we were, back to square one, the build-up to the World Cup which had started so well shattered. Undoubtedly the defeat was a shocking blow to Scotland's morale and a sickening start to Willie Ormond, who said: 'This was a terrible blow. I must sleep on this—if sleep I can— before I get down to sorting things out.'

But the truth had to be faced. England had out-gunned and out-classed the Scots and excuses about poor conditions and defensive mistakes were no consolation.

It seemed to me that Scotland needed taller and bigger players, for too often the wee boys in blue looked like Cairn terriers snapping fruitlessly at the heels of giants.

It was a dismal start to the centenary celebrations for the night before Scotland had lost 2–1 to England in the Under-23 international at Rugby Park. Certainly England had blown out every one of the 100 candles on the SFA birthday cake and we were left singing the Centenary Blues.

Perhaps it is time we paid more attention to the Under-23 scene, played more games at this level with foreign sides and had the youngsters together for solid training. After all, our record against England is significant. England have won seven to Scotland's meagre two, five have been drawn and one was abandoned with Young England well ahead.

I am convinced that it is from the young sides we find the stars to give us a first-class top international team. We haven't had that for a long time—perhaps because not enough time and attention have been paid to the Under-23s.

It wasn't the end of the world, of course, for we have grown accustomed to international football disaster and it didn't really spell the end of hopes for the World Cup in Munich—but it was a distressing start to the centenary celebrations and it was a new Flodden.

Scots hate to lose to England, no matter what pundits say about victories over Brazil and West Germany, for instance, being much more important nowadays. And that's what made the centenary game so disappointing.

Celtic's 6000th milestone

I T was fitting that Celtic's 6000th Scottish League goal should be scored by Bobby Murdoch. No Celt in modern times more deserved the honour for Murdoch has been one of the truly great players, a credit to his club and country, a real artist.

The goal was scored on 10 February 1973, against Partick Thistle at Parkhead and while it was not one in the typical Murdoch thunderbolt manner—coming as it did following a goal-mouth scramble —it brought a magic moment to the club, always famed for their tremendous scoring exploits.

It's a proud moment for Bobby Murdoch— and a moment for remembrance at Parkhead. It's a get-together of the 'Goal in a Thousandth' club in the Parkhead trophy room. Bobby is the latest member. He scored Celtic's 6000th goal against Partick Thistle in February, 1973 and here you see him receiving congratulations from the other members of a notable club . . .

Adam McLean, who scored Celtic's 2000th goal, Jimmy McGrory, who notched the 3000th and Jimmy Delaney, the man who marked up Parkhead's 4000th. The scorer of the 5000th Celtic goal, Frank Brogan, was absent through illness.

What a milestone this was in the history of the club. After all, the Scottish League did not start until 1890–91 and that they were the first club to reach the total of 6000 shows that Celtic are second to none in the art of popping the ball into the net —the art spectators love most of all.

Today Bobby Murdoch plays with repose, with skill and artistry. But he earned his international caps and the admiration of the fans because of a more explosive style and he found wing-half was the ideal position in which to exploit bubbling energy, pace and breath-taking shooting.

When the international programme started in 1965–66, Murdoch had given little thought to playing for Scotland. After all, we were rich in wing-halves— Dave Mackay, Pat Crerand, Jim Baxter, John Greig, Billy Bremner, Billy Stevenson.

Yet his aggressive play had been noted by the selectors and when injury struck and John Greig was fielded at back against Italy at Hampden, Murdoch was brought into Scotland's team and became an instant success.

He still has a vital part to play for Celtic and few surpass him when it comes to slinging accurate passes to all parts of the pitch.

He follows in famous footsteps—those of Alec McNair, Adam McLean, Jimmy McGrory, Jimmy Delaney and Frank Brogan.

McNair was the scorer of Celtic's 1000th goal and this immortal Alec scored it against Motherwell at Fir Park on 18 January 1908.

It was a long shot from 40 yards and a 2–0 win over Motherwell put Celtic into third place behind Falkirk and Dundee in the race for the league title. Celtic went on to win the flag for the fourth time in a row. They also took the Scottish, Glasgow and Charity Cups to become the first club to win every major honour in one season. The team was: Adams, McLeod, Weir, Young, McNair, Mitchell, Bennett, McMenemy, McLean, Somers, Hamilton.

Celtic's 2000th goal was scored by famous winger Adam McLean on 12 February, 1921, and it came with a fine shot just before the interval at Parkhead. Celtic won 6–0 that day and the team was: Shaw, Livingstone, Glasgow, Gilchrist, Murphy, McMaster, McAtee, Gallagher, McInally, McFarlane, McLean.

Who else but sharpshooting Jimmy McGrory, then at the height of his fine career, could have notched Celtic's 3000th goal? This goal was also scored against Motherwell at Fir Park, on 12 March 1933, on this occasion. Although Motherwell won 4–2, McGrory had the honour of scoring the historic goal 15 minutes from the end. Team: Wallace, Hogg, McGonagle, Wilson, McDonald, Hughes, R. Thomson, Napier, McGrory, F. O'Donnell, H. O'Donnell.

Another outstanding Celt, Jimmy Delaney, was the man who marked up the club's 4000th goal. Celtic beat Morton 2–1 at Parkhead and Delaney got a neat goal after typical build-up work. Team: Miller, Hogg, P. McDonald, Lynch, McMillan, McAuley, Delaney, Kiernan, J. Gallacher, W. Gallacher, O'Sullivan. The date was 25 November 1945.

The 5000th goal was scored by Frank Brogan on 4 April 1962, when Celtic beat Partick Thistle 2–1 at Firhill. It was beautifully taken, the winger running onto a Pat Crerand free kick and cracking the ball high into the net. Team: Haffey, Donnelly, Kennedy, Crerand, McNeill, Clark, Brogan, Chalmers, Hughes, Divers, Byrne.

And now Celtic, princes of goal-scoring, set out on the trail of their 7000th goal.

Where have all the centre-forwards gone?

ONCE it was the ambition of every aspiring footballer to be a centre-forward, a star in the glamour position, the place in which you earned the highest fame.

For centre-forwards were the super men of their day. Men such as Jimmy McGrory, Barney Battles, Willie Thornton, Hughie Gallacher and Lawrie Reilly captured nearly all the goals. They were the heroes, they were the players all the schoolboys wanted to copy.

But things have changed. Football has become obsessed with team play which has phased out the fabulous leaders and robbed the game of its heroes. Scoring today happens more as the result of team effort rather than individual ability.

Much of the glamour has departed. There are no idols for the fans to worship and I feel that the game has lost much of its attraction.

Now all the kids want to be mid-field players.

One of the reasons for the decline of the centre-forward is that in the old days the leaders of the line battled essentially with centre-halves and their goals came mainly

The dash of Colin Stein, once of Hibs and Rangers, and now with Coventry . . .

from victories in those hectic man-to-man battles. With the coming of the sweeper and the second centre-half, however, the space behind centre-halves which the men in the No 9 shirts used so well disappeared.

Now we have double strikers, layers-off and target men. Teams have become machines . . . they score goals like machines . . . but the fans prefer to watch real men.

With the decline of the centre-forward, the buccaneer, the husky athlete who could race like a deer, head the ball with acrobatic grace and shoot with the velocity of a machine-gun, romance went out of football.

And with the disappearance of the type of leader of the late 1930's and late 40's— the intellectuals who fancied clever pattern play but were still individualists— artistry also vanished.

Now strikers are told to lean on defenders, hammer them, keep them busy, so that others can sneak up from behind and get the goals that come from mistakes made as the hefty hatchet-men batter in, relying more on power than skill.

So the strikers have no glamour. Only ingloriously and indirectly do they decide matches.

The man with the ferocious shot, however, is still the footballer the crowds love to watch most. That's why Scotland's Peter Lorimer is such a favourite. He hits the ball tremendously hard.

Yet Leeds United don't really play Peter as a main attacker. In the old days, he would certainly have been a centre-forward and probably one of the most famous. In these modern times, he lurks on the fringes, waiting for a chance to use his power after strikers Alan Clark and Mick Jones have softened up the defenders.

66

The slick scoring of Joe Harper, transferred from Aberdeen to Everton . . .

The all-out action of Lou
Macari, who has joined
Manchester United from Celtic.

Such is the changing face of football.

If I were a manager, I would want to make the player with the best shot my main striker. So I would probably create a new record for swift firing even in a trade which is notorious for the short-term stay of the man in the world's hottest seat, the managerial chair.

Perhaps, however, it's modern football that's crazy, not me. For instance, the player with the most thundering shot is—a goalkeeper.

Down at Largs in November 1972, just before Scotland's World Cup game with Denmark, a special test was arranged to see who was our champion sharpshooter.

And it was Leeds United goalkeeper David Harvey, who had just received his first international cap for Scotland, who won. His best shot was timed at a speed of 75·6 mph, which beat the British record of 74·9 set up in 1966 at Birmingham by Harvey's team-mate, Lorimer (who didn't take part in the Largs test because of an injury).

The test was conducted by dynamics experts from Glasgow's Strathclyde University and the flight of the ball was recorded over a measured distance by cine camera.

Second in the speed test was Asa Hartford, of West Bromwich Albion, at 64·0 mph, third was Ken Dalglish of Celtic, at 63·2 and fourth was yet another goalkeeper, Alistair Hunter, of Kilmarnock, at 62·5.

Well, wouldn't you think that if you were boss of Leeds you would be playing Harvey and Lorimer as the strikers?

I repeat: This is football today . . . strikers are bustlers, not crackshots.

I still prefer a real centre-forward—and I don't care whether he scores with whistling shots or neatly placed flicks.

And there were leaders who got goals because they knew exactly where they should hit the ball to and relied on placing, not velocity.

The greatest centre-forward of the 70's is undoubtedly Germany's Gerd Muller. He's an individualist—and he gives the lie to experts who say we need double strikers, who sneer that old-fashioned leaders are out of date.

Muller looks to me like a new Lawrie Reilly. Better than the Hibs and Scotland man? Probably. Because Muller can hit the ball hard and also place it perfectly.

Only one athlete, I believe, would be better than Muller. That's Muhammad Ali—the man who won fame by clouting

Derek Johnstone, of Rangers, who is a versatile young man. Now he stars at centre-half but not so long ago he looked as though he was about to become a tremendous centre-forward.

opponents in the boxing ring and not foot-balls—and I think he would have been a fine striker in soccer because he was the prince of prodders, an expert jabber. And I maintain that the centre-forward who can slickly push the ball into the net is as effective as the player with a tremendous shot.

Nowadays attackers, in the press of strong defence, don't really have time to draw back a leg and shoot. The man who matters is the player who has such strength in his leg, as Clay alias Ali has in his arms, that he can prod the ball quickly and powerfully over the line.

Certainly Lawrie Reilly is of that opinion. He told me: 'It's the push that matters most. It's almost fatal in football today to bring your leg back to hit the ball fiercely—for someone's sure to whip the ball . . . or your leg . . . away before you can hit it'.

Lawrie was a master of the prod and when you think back on the goals he scored for Hibs and Scotland you realise just what strength he had in his legs.

What do goalkeepers, who should know, think about this theory? Let me go back down memory lane again to recall a conversation I had with Jimmy Brown, then with Kilmarnock. He was Scotland's most colourful keeper.

Said Jimmy: 'The forward who worries me most is the fellow with the strong leg who can poke the ball into the net. You can't see him making his move to shoot and that can be fatal for the keeper.

'I think, on the other hand, that most capable goalies should be able to save the fierce shot for he can usually see the ball coming as well as sensing the forward going through all the motions of drawing back his foot to make his kick'.

In those days, no-one was better at putting the ball in the net than that fabulous

Ken Mackie, Dunfermline Athletic's teenager, who is attracting envious English eyes.

character, Handy Andy Kerr. And not always with explosive drives, though Andy could lash the ball with the best. He scored for Partick Thistle and Kilmarnock, among others, with leg, shoulder, head, back—and behind.

I recall a centre-half saying to me: "See that yin Kerr? For 80 minutes you never notice him. Then he scores a goal. And I'll tell you something . . . he's most dangerous when he's sitting on his behind'.

So he was.

Alas, there's no variety nowadays, few characters among the centre-forwards.

As always, Scotland has plenty of great young players. But how many of them are promising centre-forwards?

There's Kenny Dalglish, of Celtic, of course. He is the best prospect in this country. He's versatile. He may become a new Bobby Murdoch in mid-field. But I consider his best position is up front—as a centre-forward.

But where are the others? Young Ken Mackie, of Dunfermline, is promising. So is Jim McCabe, of Motherwell. And Derek Parlane, of Rangers, is one of the bravest young strikers in the game. Alas, it's a short list.

Let's hope, however, that football changes again, provides once more the old excitement, the old room for manoeuvre.

Kenny Dalglish, of Celtic, who promises to be the best of them all . . .

Let's hope the game will produce soon some of the more glamorous individualists, men like the old-timers who made soccer the most exciting game on earth.

Let's hope Scotland allows more scope to the individuals, especially the centre-forwards, than is shown in other countries where players have to conform to stern, machine-like moulding.

What would you give to see a new Jimmy McGrory, a new Willie Thornton, a new Willie Bauld?

The thought makes me weep . . .

70

SUPER SAVES

Scottish fans may not see as many super saves as they used to in the good old days, according to Hugh Taylor.

But that's not to say our modern keepers have a quiet time in every match.

Anything but.

And, as these dramatic pictures show, we still have goalies who can bring off saves as magnificent as any made by their illustrious predecessors in the good old days.

. . . Even if they're not called on to make as many . . .

OK, OK, it's my ball, says Dumbarton keeper Willie Whigham as he makes an unusual save in a match against Celtic.

NOT enough goals! Too much mid-field play! That's the cry in these modern times as football becomes more sophisticated, more computerised. Well, of course, we'd all like to see more goals. But I'm afraid something else is fast departing from the current soccer scene. . . .

Great saves!

It's true. How often nowadays do we applaud a save which borders on the miraculous? How often do we see a goal-keeper stop a shot or header which has the forward shaking his head in disbelief?

Not often enough.

It's part of the new trend. More and more defenders are stopping attackers getting in shots. So well-drilled are the rearguards that keepers seem to be in action only when pulling down crosses or clearing corner kicks.

Certainly now and again a goalkeeper

Fewer keepers are quicker off their marks than Bobby Clark, of Aberdeen, who is seen here diving to his team's rescue just in time as Lou Macari, then with Celtic, bores in.

makes a breath-taking save to show that he is as agile, as skilful as his predecessors —and there is no doubt that goalies such as Bobby Clark, of Aberdeen, Thomson Allan, of Dundee, Peter McCloy, of Rangers, Alistair Hunter, of Celtic, Jim Stewart, of Kilmarnock, Dave Gorman, of East Fife and a few more are as capable as any of the princes of the past.

Somehow, however, great saves don't make the headlines any more—and we have to drift down memory lane to re-capture the thrills which used to make the keeper the hero of the day.

Wipe your eyes, then, fellow veterans —and prepare to have your eyes really opened, youngsters, as we live again the tremendous saves which broke the attackers' hearts.

Perhaps the most historic save was made away back in 1928 in the Scottish Cup Final between Rangers and Celtic. Certainly it was one of the most vital— and I always think that a save should really only become famous when it leads to a team's victory.

In that respect, the save made by big Tom Hamilton all those years ago was important and in Rangers' centenary celebrations in 1973 it should be recalled in all its glory.

For the Hamilton save, made even more memorable because it was captured in all its high drama by a *Daily Record* photographer of that era, won a prize and became probably the best-known football picture of all time, could be said to have taken Rangers to a new peak of triumph.

Just after the first world war, there was a hoodoo over Ibrox. In 1928 they were again in the cup final, but their fans were anxious. Rangers hadn't won the cup for 25 years, although they had appeared five times in the final since they last took the trophy, beating Hearts in 1903.

And in the 1928 match Celtic opened with a tremendous burst. With only a few minutes gone it looked a goal all the way for Celtic as . . .

A terrific first-time shot by Connolly blurred the ball as the Celtic winger hammered it at goal.

But big Tom Hamilton from Renton hurled himself like a rocket across his line

Just in time—and Dave Stewart, of Ayr United, gets down to stop a shot from Celtic's Tommy Callaghan.

and got not one but both hands to the ball and made a save in a million—a save which will never be forgotten by all who saw it, a save which gave Rangers the confidence and inspiration they needed to beat their cup hoodoo.

As the late Dave Meiklejohn, who was Rangers' captain that day, told me later: 'That save did the trick for us. It looked a certain goal but Tom Hamilton brought off a miracle. We knew then we could win —and we did'.

Hamilton had to make many more brilliant saves before Rangers took command —but none equalled the magnificence of

Opposite: A helping hand for Stirling goalkeeper Young? Not on your life. Willie Johnstone, now with West Bromwich Albion, is trying to make things easier for himself and Rangers. But the keeper wins.

Below: Lucky Ayr—they've more than one outstanding goalie. Also making a name for himself is young Ally McLean. Here you see why as he pushes a shot round the post.

This time it's Celtic's keeper, Evan Williams, in action and he grasps the ball at the last possible second.

that stop from Connolly. Celtic hearts dropped—and in the end Rangers won 4–0.

Thanks first to Tom Hamilton's save in a million.

Ironically, the save I remember best was also breath-taking—but this time it was a save which led to Rangers' downfall. Also in the Scottish Cup Final. Exactly a year after they thought Tom Hamilton had sent their hoodoo running.

In 1929 Rangers started hot favourites.

This time it's Celtic's keeper, Evan Williams, in action and he grasps the ball at the last possible second.

No wonder. Kilmarnock, who had fought so gallantly to reach Hampden, were in trouble, with nearly half a team injured and their eleven a combination of ageing players and callow youths. Rangers, on the other hand, were again the greatest team in Scotland. What chance had a team packed with reserves of winning the Cup?

At the start, it looked as though Kilmarnock had no chance. Rangers, with the wind behind them, as Celtic had enjoyed in the previous year's final, set up savage assaults on the Ayrshire goal.

Only to find Sam Clemie in superlative form, making one glorious save after another.

But in the 17th minute it seemed that even a keeper as heroic as the lithe man from Lugar would have to admit defeat.

Who was the greatest?

. . . At last a Rangers player was away on his own. Jock Buchanan. Boring through relentlessly, past all the Kilmarnock defenders. Only Clemie to beat. And a frantic lunge by Killie's Hugh Morton. Buchanan sprawling. Penalty!

Tommy Craig walked slowly up to take the kick. Clemie spat on his hands, hurled his cap into the back of the net and crouched.

Craig ran forward leisurely and hit a tremendous shot, a fast, accurate shot, flying to the right of the goal. Again—it seemed a scorer all the way.

Except to Clemie. Sam soared away to his right and he had the ball and all the Ayrshire fans went mad over another save of the century.

Again an inspiring save. Again a save that led to victory. For Kilmarnock's patched-up team took fire, and trampled the mighty Rangers into a 2–0 defeat.

Thanks to that brilliant Clemie save.

In their day, Hamilton and Clemie were more than competent goalkeepers and if they were never in the top echelon they have achieved undying fame by their dramatic saves on the big occasion.

Who was the greatest Scottish keeper? Jimmy Cowan, of Morton? Jerry Dawson, of Rangers? John Thomson, of Celtic? All were superb.

Perhaps it was the ill-fated Thomson, however, who made the greatest single save of these three—and it was fantastic because Thomson, signed as an 18-year-old from Wellesley Juniors away back in 1926–27, made saves which were unbelievable.

Indeed, it would be hard to exaggerate Thomson's magical skill and his admirers to this day declare that neither before nor since have they seen a keeper so swift, so elegant, so superbly safe in operation. He had, according to one chronicler, 'the spring of a jaguar and the effortless grace of a skimming sparrow'.

His super save? According to that great Celtic centre-forward, Jimmy McGrory, it was at Parkhead against Kilmarnock. The man who shot was 'Peerie' Cunningham, a centre-forward whose shots, taken on the pivot, left either foot with a velocity that equalled that of Peter Lorimer nowadays. But Peerie was cunning . . . he could bend his drives.

Anyhow . . . Cunningham that day at Parkhead hit the ball in such a way that it seemed certain to go for the right-hand post.

Thomson dived for it in that direction. Almost on the instant, he divined his mistake. The ball switched towards the left-hand post. In mid-air, John Thomson twisted, hurled himself across the goal and got the tips of his fingers to the ball to turn it round the post.

'We stood open-mouthed,' said Jimmy McGrory afterwards.

Yes, all who saw Thomson recall numerous instances of his mystic skill. He was a brilliant virtuoso and if he hadn't died so tragically that dreadful day in Sep-

A thrill from an Old Firm tussle as Rangers' Peter McCloy grips the ball securely with Ken Dalglish of Celtic running in.

tember 1931, he would undoubtedly have become the greatest goalkeeper of all time. Many say he is.

In recent times, the man who emulated Tom Hamilton and Sam Clemie was Eddie Connachan, of Dunfermline Athletic.

And his performance in the cup final of 1961 will go down in glowing letters in the history of super saves.

Celtic were favourites to beat Dunfermline—an old story. And they might have, too, if it hadn't been for a Connachan save.

In 30 minutes, Celtic's John Hughes beat three Athletic defenders, then passed to Steve Chalmers, the attacker with the devastating shot. Always alert round goal,

Steve hit his shot hard to the junction of the post and bar. The keeper was unsighted.

But with a pantherish leap Eddie Connachan was up from nowhere to clutch the ball as all Fife cheered a super save.

So Athletic were inspired and earned a 0–0 draw. And in the replay another defiant display by Connachan helped the Fifers to take the cup by beating Celtic 2–0.

I don't think, though, that anyone will contest the display of Jimmy Cowan

79

Opposite: Ouch, mind my back —is that what Airdrie keeper Roddy McKenzie is saying as he punches the ball away from Dundee United's Kenny Cameron?

against England at Wembley as the greatest ever seen by a goalkeeper in an international match.

Jimmy made not one save in a million. He made dozens!

It was in 1949 that the Morton keeper gave his immortal display. Inside the first ten minutes with England pressing eagerly he had made at least four spell-binding saves, one in particular at point-blank range from Stanley Mortensen being hailed as the greatest since the war.

His brilliance gave Scotland such confidence that they won 3-1, though most people had felt England had such a fine side that year that they would have achieved a handsome victory. They might have, too—if it hadn't been for Jimmy Cowan.

Jimmy was carried shoulder-high from the pitch at the end—and the next night more than 10,000 fans turned out at a Glasgow station to give him an ovation as he returned with his team-mates on the Royal Scot.

All these wonderful goalies provided tremendous thrills.

Let's hope that our soccer becomes more exciting and that the lads of today, the Clarks, McCloys, Allans, Stewarts, Roughs, McAlpines and rest, get more chances to show they can be as magnificent as any of their illustrious predecessors.

Another great young Scottish keeper is Alan Rough, of Partick Thistle, saving in a match against Celtic.

Secret from the past takes Hibs to League Cup glory

EVEN in this modern age of football, an age in which the game seems to have a transistor instead of a heart and computerised robots instead of gay cavaliers, the ideas from the past can still work.

Hibernian proved this when they won the Scottish League Cup at Hampden by beating Celtic 2–1 on the gusty, dripping afternoon of 9 December 1972. They ended a heart-breaking, 20-year spell in the soccer wilderness because their manager, Eddie Turnbull, pinned his faith in the audacious attacking plans which had made the Famous Five of Easter Road Scotland's most brilliant front-line in the 1950's.

Away back in 1959, Turnbull was saying: 'I have often been asked what was the secret of the success of the Hibs attack of Gordon Smith, Bobby Johnstone, Lawrie Reilly, Willie Ormond and myself. To my mind it was this: There was always one of us going out of position. Yes, even into defence—in fact, anywhere into the open.

'I was generally the rover. But not always. Part of our plan was to bamboozle the opposition. And this worked because

my colleagues had an uncanny sense of position. We always seemed to know where a mate would be, no matter how far out of position he had wandered. The main reason for all the wandering was to lure defenders out of position.

'Wandering caught an opponent in two minds. He didn't know whether to follow the man he was supposed to be marking—and thus leave a gap into which another Hibernian player could run to get the pass. If he left me, for instance, alone, I could get the ball.

'In my creed, possession is nine points of the football law.'

It still is. And Turnbull's ideas helped Hibs to beat Celtic. Hibs were once again the masters of the open space.

Nevertheless, Celtic started the match as favourites. Yet such was the attraction of the final that a crowd of 71,696 turned up on a nasty day to see two fine teams who had become the top two in Scotland. Already Celtic had lost to Hibernian at Hampden in the final of the Drybrough Cup—on 5 August in an astonishing contest which ended 5–3 in Hib's favour. A

The goal which put Hibernian on the road to glory. The falling Pat Stanton scores following a neat free-kick.

few months before, however, Hibernian had been at their least impressive against Celtic in the Scottish Cup Final—and had lost 6–1.

Both clubs wanted desperately to win. Hibernian had taken honours in the Summer Cup and the Drybrough Cup but they hadn't won a real national honour since their League Championship flag in 1951–52, the era of the Famous Five. And it was 70 years since they had triumphed in a national knock-out tournament—their victory in the Scottish Cup Final of 1902 when they defeated Celtic 1–0.

Celtic, however, also wanted to end a wait. It was their 11th appearance in the League Cup Final, their ninth in a row—and also their 94th League Cup-tie without a break since August 1964. Yet although they had won the Cup on seven occasions—a record they shared with Rangers—they had lost the two previous finals to Partick Thistle and Rangers.

Celtic had reached the final by winning their League Cup section in which were also Stirling Albion, East Fife and Arbroath, beating Stranraer in the second round, finally vanquishing Dundee in the quarter-final after three games and putting Aberdeen out in the semi-final. They had scored 35 goals and lost 15.

Hibernian had won their section, in which their rivals were Aberdeen Queen's Park and Queen of the South, defeated Dundee United in the second round, Airdrie in the quarter-final and Rangers in the semi-final. They had scored 30 goals and lost 13.

Celtic were fancied by the bookmakers, the neutrals and most of the critics.

But Hibernian had their secret from the past. . . .

This was how the teams lined up at Hampden:

Celtic — Williams, McGrain, Brogan, McCluskey, McNeill, Hay, Johnstone, Connelly, Dalglish, Hood, Macari. Sub: Callaghan.

Hibs—Herriot, Brownlie, Schaedler, Stanton, Black, Blackley, Edwards, O'Rourke, Gordon, Cropley, Duncan. Sub: Hamilton.

Referee was A. McKenzie, of Larbert.

The match began predictably, with Celtic taking command and Hibs looking nervous. After all, Hibs had played miserably although winning against Rangers in the League Cup semi-final at Hampden whereas Celtic were superb on the huge ground against Dundee and Aberdeen. So Hibs were caught in possession and too often their passes went astray.

The man who restored Hibs' faith in themselves was John Brownlie, who had been said to have taken a severe injury not long before the final. He didn't show it, however, and quickly he realised he had the beating of Jimmy Johnstone, that superb winger who had been given the unusual role of playing against the enthusiastic, talented back, whose forte was spectacular overlapping.

It wasn't a role Johnstone appreciated and lack of his right-wing raiding cost Celtic dear as the wee man ran haplessly on the left, fruitlessly trying to stop the galloping Brownlie, who defended stoutly and yet found time to romp into attack.

Still, Celtic had the early command and they should have taken the lead in the 18th minute when Lou Macari, all on his own, rose to a Harry Hood cross—but headed over the bar.

Then Pat Stanton, that great captain of Hibs, began to impress his stamp on the game, which developed into an equal contest, more interesting, frankly, than exciting because defences were on top and goal-mouth incidents few.

If Celtic went near again when their

83

A goal for the memory book. A brilliant header by Jim O'Rourke puts Hibs two up in spectacular fashion at Hampden.

most attractive move ended with Ken Dalglish, another magnificent player in the wind and rain, firing in a fierce shot which Jim Herriot saved confidently, their opponents also contributed a bright attack during which Billy McNeill was forced to give goalkeeper Evan Williams a fright, passing back so narrowly that the ball edged the post by inches.

Then came the first big thrill. From the corner kick, Stanton raced in to head powerfully. It looked a goal—until Evan Williams, so often merely an onlooker in the Celtic net as his team takes complete command, showed his brilliance with a fine save.

The first half, though, was sadly short of incident and the game had hardly lived up to pre-match expectations. Indeed, that first 45 minute session was in keeping with the drabness of the League Cup of 1972. Usually this tournament is one of the brightest. It was run on the principle of

eight sections of four clubs, four of the sections consisting of First Division clubs —and one section of five clubs. This caused a supplementary tie and then came the exciting part, the games among the section qualifiers.

But there had been a clamour for seeding and it was decided that the seeded clubs should be the top four from the First and Second Divisions. It was also decided that the two top teams in each section go forward to the second round.

But the idea was a flop. The fans weren't happy. So more people deserted the already gaping terracings.

No wonder everyone in Scottish soccer was hoping the final would bring back some of the glamour.

In the end, it did.

For the second half at Hampden was memorable, a feast of football . . . though we could have done without incidents at the interval which brought spectators racing for safety as missiles were thrown at one end.

The second half belonged to Hibs.

And one of the reasons for that was that manager Turnbull recalled the plan of the

Famous Five, decided some of his players had been too static and would have to move out of position.

He said afterwards: 'I made half-time changes because we had been playing far too tight. Passes were going amiss and some of our lads were nervous and careless.

'I felt it was ridiculous not to use Hampden's wide open spaces so I made changes.

'I believed we had the skill to take over the mid-field area and to win the final if these men made the room to move in. To that end I told Alex Edwards to switch from his mid-field role to the right wing, Arthur Duncan to go back to the left wing and Pat Stanton to move up.'

There was new heart in the Hibs players as they began the second half against the wind—for they had become renowned as a side who improved after half-time, thanks to the fine reading of the game and instructions of their manager.

Yet—it was Celtic who should have opened the scoring in a dramatic spell.

Fifty-six minutes had gone. Once again Dalglish, an outstanding Celt, made an opening. A gorgeous pass let Harry Hood through. The Glasgow fans began to cheer. Hood was all on his own. Herriot alone barred his path.

Steadily, however, the keeper advanced. Hood shot. But the ball cannoned off the body of Herriot and spun to safety.

A grand chance was lost, a fine save was made.

A goal then—and Celtic might have gone to town, repeated their victory of the Scottish Cup Final over their opponents . . . despite all the hard talking that had gone on in the Hibs dressing room during the interval.

Hibs breathed again—and set off on a magnificent attacking spree of their own. It was the 60th minute. A free-kick was given to Hibernian just outside the penalty area. The referee decided McNeill had fouled Gordon. That decision didn't go down well with the Celtic skipper or the fans from Parkhead—and, indeed, it looked as though the Hibs centre-forward had caused the infringement. But the referee was on the spot and in tough tussles when two players go for a ball in the air it is often a lottery as to who is given the foul. So a free-kick for Hibs it was.

And what magnificent use of that award they made.

Celtic's only goal was scored by Kenny Dalglish. It was a magnificent effort—but it wasn't enough to stop Hibs.

Above: A narrow escape for
Celtic as Hibs press furiously.

Opposite: Celtic's Evan
Williams makes a fine save in
the League Cup Final.

Cunningly Alex Edwards lobbed the ball over the Celtic wall of anxious defenders. And what a gap there was behind them—a gap magnificently exploited by Pat Stanton. The Hibs skipper had moved smoothly into position, bamboozled two opponents and still had the ball.

His low shot beat Evan Williams and briskly hit the back of the net—to give Hibernian a vital goal.

Six minutes later, the Edinburgh club's idea of allowing their players to wander paid off again—with a really glorious goal.

This time Stanton was away out on the right wing. He took a fine pass from Edwards. For a moment he studied the situation, saw Alan Gordon at the far post and coolly whipped over a beautiful cross. The Celtic defenders hesitated again. They had an eye on Gordon. As they waited, in sailed Jim O'Rourke—at the near post—beat everyone with his leap and put his side two up with a spectacular flying header.

No-one, however, can ever count Celtic out. Two goals in six minutes would have staggered any other side. Not those valiant Celts. They hit back ferociously.

Although lucky to be only two down, for the immaculate Stanton had hit the post soon after O'Rourke's goal, McNeill had cleared on the line and Williams had dropped a Stanton header as Hibs turned on the style. Celtic refused to give in.

And because of a combination of Hibs' determination to stay on the attack and Celtic's pride, the enthralling League Cup Final ended dramatically.

Long-striding Tom Callaghan had come on for the frustrated Johnstone. Celtic were trying desperately to get back into the attack.

And in 76 minutes fortune smiled on the Parkhead men. Out of the worried Celtic defence came a long ball. In a flash, the young Celt had it under control and off he dashed on a fine 50-yard run towards Herriot. The keeper came out to narrow the angle but Dalglish kept his head, pulled back his leg—and shot neatly past the keeper.

Celtic were back in the game again. And what a frantic finish there was as they stormed in for the equaliser.

Hibs, however, were unwilling to merely try to hold out—and, indeed, both teams made chances in the hectic closing stage.

Then—the whistle. And Hibs had won a wonderful 2–1 victory, to make themselves again a power in the land, give them fresh confidence and win a national trophy at last.

No-one could grudge the players their minutes of joy as they ran to the corner of the ground where most of their supporters were gathered and give them a victory wave.

Certainly the 71,696 fans who had braved the weather had enjoyed a match which did great honour to Scottish football.

Celtic manager Jock Stein summed it up sportingly and accurately: 'Hibs were the better team on the day—that's what happened,' he said.

It was Hibernian's first League Cup victory in the history of the competition and a quick breakthrough for manager Turnbull, who had joined his old club from Aberdeen as boss only in July, 1971.

Eddie was a member of the Hibs side which won the League championship three times in five years. But that 'Famous Five' Hibs side never won a cup.

Nevertheless, it was Turnbull's secret from that glorious period which had helped the new Hibs to win the League Cup so well.

The football pitch is a stage . . .

. . . And all the players are actors. Well, are they? Some, we allege when they don't play their parts as we expect them to, are more suited to be comics than footballers.

Some, we declare, should receive Oscars for performances in deceiving the referee, crying out to high heaven that they have been mortally wounded and in pathetically maintaining their innocence when they are held to have digressed.

There is no doubt, however, that all human emotions are revealed in football by players —and fans—in a way most actors would envy.

For example . . .

ADMIRATION is shown by this young lady for Kenny Dalglish, of Celtic. She's a student who 'shadowed' the brilliant young Celt at the kick-in during a Charity Day Saturday.

DESPERATION is written all over the face of St
Johnstone goalkeeper Donaldson as he tries to clear
during a match with Morton.

CONCENTRATION is the name of the game for these Rangers' backroom boys pictured during a match—Joe Craven, Tom Craig, Stan Anderson, Willie Thornton and manager Jock Wallace.

CONDEMNATION—of each other—makes Arbroath
defenders bitter indeed after they've lost a goal to
Partick Thistle.

INDIGNATION at a tackle by Aberdeen's Willie Young
is revealed by Dixie Deans, of Celtic.

CONSOLATION is given to Rangers' back Sandy Jardine
by goalkeeper Peter McCloy following an injury.

GESTICULATION—well, that seems rather a tame word for it—by Motherwell's Willie McCallum helps to put Rangers' Tommy McLean off his stride.

Elegance is the name of George's game

THE choice of George Connelly, Celtic's master of all the soccer arts and crafts, as the Scottish football writers' Player of the Year in season 1972–73 poses an engrossing question: Isn't it time for a renaissance in the game?

This is hardly the age of football elegance. It is the era of the all-purpose player, the bustler, the hustler, the buzzing mid-field dynamo, all power and thrust and red-hot action. Action is often torrid, if not downright vicious. Method is king, drill is all.

Yet this is not what the critics want— or the fans. They want the velvet approach, the cheeky touch, the air of cool command. We Scots really prefer the Baxters and their icy disdain of husky tearaways who try to tackle them, the courtlier football in which real skill rather than fervour brought success.

The proof of this is shown in recent winners of the Player of the Year award.

George Connelly receives a kiss from daughter Sharon after winning the Player of the Year title.

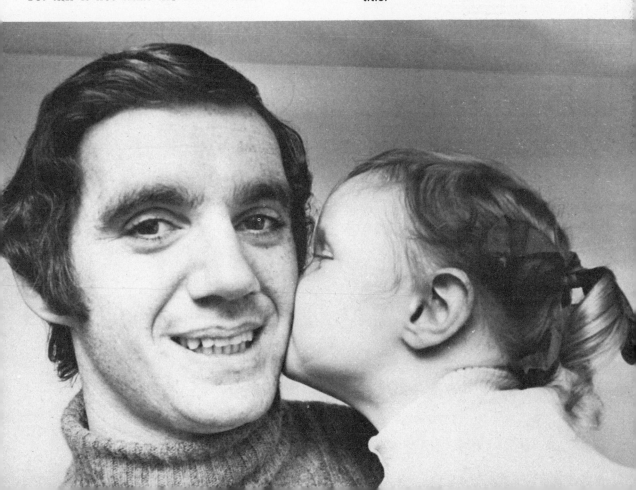

No one surpasses Connelly in brilliant footballing confections. And he follows another outstanding artist who prefers subtlety to savagery, Dave Smith, of Rangers. The year before Smith, it was Martin Buchan, of Aberdeen now Manchester United, who took the title—another marvellously polished performer.

Ironically, all these players are defenders—yet players who have poise and personality, who rely on sheer ability, contemptuously scorn the desperate touch or tackle and match in flair any of the great attackers of the past, the Gordon Smiths, the Alan Mortons, the Jimmy Masons.

Would it not, then, bring new hope for football if more emphasis on the cultured were put also today on attackers? Would the game not improve if once again we had wing-halves of contrast, say the surge of Bobby Evans and the calculating probing of Jim Baxter, and ball artists up front, instead of relying on packed middle lines and robot-like tactics which leave no room for delicacy, the finer touches and the magical moves of the past we still drool over?

Certainly it would be much more attractive. But I doubt if it will happen. The price of fear is too high. Safety is all nowadays. Few clubs allow their ball players freedom of action. It's the numbers game, the day of close and zonal marking, the biggest worry, fear of the unorthodox.

Let us be thankful, then, that we still have players such as Connelly, who is Scotland's Beckenbauer, an able defender yet a key man in his team's attacks because of wonderfully precise passes which he dispatches from his own penalty area to cause havoc among the ranks of opponents.

An old-fashioned player is George. In some ways. In breath-taking ball control—he once earned cheers at Parkhead when as a youngster he played 'keepy-up' to

A much younger George Connelly, his picture taken not long after he arrived at Parkhead as a slim 16-year-old from Valleyfield. He was famous then, though, for he could juggle the ball 2,000 times without letting it hit the ground.

entertain the fans before a big match—and in his love of the game. In other ways he is as modern as a transistor. For his role was never used in the past. It is a variation dreamed up by that master of tactics, Celtic manager Jock Stein. Connelly stands beside centre-half Billy McNeill—but not merely as an aide, a stopper, a sweeper. Construction is the name of George's game.

And no one is better at it than the tall young man from Fife. No, not even the great Beckenbauer, now growing weary after an illustrious career. Connelly combines the pass ability of a Crerand with the magnificent reading of the game of a Bobby Moore and he has Patsy Gallagher's fantastic control. In short, you could call him a tall Alex James for he plays a similar role to that of the late, great Arsenal wizard —but he directs his arrows from the rear not the front or middle as Alex did.

Connelly hails from Fife, where so many famous footballers were born and a county from which Celtic took so many outstanding players.

The transition from frail schoolboy to stalwart Celt began for Connelly when he was 14 and playing for his school on Saturday mornings.

George's older brother was the first to realise the potential in that slim frame. He talked to officials for the Junior team, Tulliallan Thistle and a call was made at the Connelly home in Valleyfield. George was invited to turn out in Kirkcaldy for Thistle against Frances Colliery.

That was more than 10 years ago but George remembers practically every kick of the ball in that match—for that was the start of a dream. 'We won 3–2 and I made the winning goal', he said. He signed for Tulliallan on the bus on the way home. And young George Connelly was on the way to fame.

Allan Gordon, of Hibs, the man in deadly scoring form last season, was runner-up in the Player of the Year race.

Scouts were never far away from the Connelly lad. But Celtic were the club he wanted to join—and Celtic knew a good thing when they saw it. At 15, George was a Celt. The first time he wore the green and white was in a Combined Reserve League game against Stirling Albion. He signed professional forms in 1966.

Now he is set to become probably the most famous Celt ever signed from Fife, home of the fabulous John Thomson, Willie Fernie and so many more.

He was to fill many positions before he found his unorthodox but so-paying role beside captain Billy McNeill.

He's as modest as he was as a boy, pays notable tribute to McNeill and to manager Stein. 'The boss has been the biggest influence on my career', he said at his new home in Blantyre, Lanarkshire, a place, incidentally, where other great Celts were discovered.

His thoughts on the game he loves are simple. 'I believe football is a game primarily of skill. It's not about kickers. And Mr. Stein has always encouraged me to play plenty of football.'

It is hardly to be wondered at that this is also the philosophy of George's predecessor as Player of the Year, Dave Smith. For the elegant Ranger says: 'I just let opponents be rough and tough if they want to be. I rely on what talent I have myself to show what I can do. If I'm fouled I ignore it. It's foolish, anyhow, to retaliate.'

Second in the football writers' poll was Alan Gordon, the Hibernian centre-forward, a man who really takes goals, in contrast to Connelly, who makes them.

Gordon is, however, another distinguished player. And like Connelly he looks the part.

It's true that great footballers don't have to resemble film stars and some of the most magnificent players of all time, especially in Scotland, have been wee bowly bachles, gangling beanpoles, young old men with what looked like the wisdom and cares of the ages making even teenage faces seem haggard and wispy striplings who bend in the slightest wind.

Yet those of us who grew up with John Wayne, Gary Cooper and Gregory Peck like our heroes, in whatever sphere, to look like heroes, the silver-spurred gallants who squint into the sun as they patrol the dusty streets of Laredo. Too many players, alas for we romantics, are more like the side-kicks, the Gabby Hayes's who supply the comic relief around the old camp-fire. Too many players, if surprised in a sauna bath, would look like truants from a primary school.

But in Connelly and Gordon everything is right. The tallness. The strength. The athletic skill. The square-jawed, clean-cut look. The long stride and the cool, strong look. They fit the old hero mould.

Let's hope they signal a new era for Scotland, an era in which we can rival any other team in the world in height, weight —and skill.

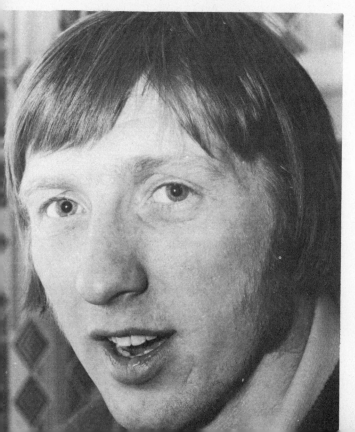

John Brownlie of Hibs, would have been a strong candidate for the title. Alas, John broke his leg during the season and was out of action for months.

A cure for our sick soccer

Take a lesson from cricket

RECONSTRUCTION—that was the name of the game in Scottish football in season 1972–73. Everyone wanted to get into the act. Everyone, it seemed, had an idea to transform the face of soccer, make it more attractive and bring back the missing millions to the terracings.

Certainly our League system is in need of a face-lift. It is unwieldy, it sorely needs streamlining. But all attempts, as always, foundered on multiplicity of interests.

Frankly, talk of reconstruction makes me yawn. I've heard it all before. Indeed, I've made suggestions for 20 years. So, of course, have scores of others. And what happened? Nothing.

Exactly 10 years ago reconstruction was also the blazing topic. Season 1962–63 had been one of the most frustrating known in the history of Scottish football. Iron winter gripped the land. By 16 February, 122 senior matches had been postponed. Reconstruction, it appeared, was essential. The officials met—and suggested a revolutionary change: summer football.

Rangers and Celtic, however, were against such a change—and rightly so. They felt a break in winter would merely drive more fans away. Once, the Glasgow Big Two felt, supporters found an alternative to football, they would stick to it and never return to the terracings. So the proposal to play soccer in the summer was thrown out. And we've never had such a bitter winter as that of 1962–63 since.

We have, however, had plenty of talk about change. For football is sick. Too many clubs are struggling. There is not enough competition.

Alas, the old, tired suggestions were made once again—a switch to three divisions, clubs to retain home gates, changes in the offside law.

There was, to be fair, a novel idea, presented by Fraser McIntosh, chairman of St. Mirren. It was bright—but not workable. It called for the League to be played in two parts, each counting as a separate competition of 17 matches in the First and 18 in the Second Division.

Then the table-toppers should play off for the championship, the bottom markers for relegation. Of course, a club topping both sections would be outright champions —a club finishing bottom both times would be relegated.

I repeat: Too many thoughts on reconstruction are just a waste of time. The fan won't be kidded. He feels he has been let down by football. He sees his club transfer one good player after another to England. He sees too many matches which mean nothing. He sees team manager Tommy Docherty put Scotland back on the international map—then suddenly leave for richer pastures. He wonders if it's worthwhile continuing to be a faithful fan.

What, actually, is wrong with football?

In Scotland, there is not enough real competition to Celtic and Rangers. Perhaps the clubs now realise they have no divine right to the automatic presence of large numbers of paying customers in an age where there is so much to do and much

101

more time for leisure. But they show few signs of doing much about it.

There is far too much hooliganism, and decent supporters are driven away by the thugs and loudmouths.

There is far too much exposure on television. There is a disgusting lack of facilities. How many clubs in this year of Moon landings, computers and other electronic marvels, provide even adequate facilities for car parking, toilets and refreshment? Precious few.

There is also far too much complacency at the top. After all, no other sport, never mind business, receives such slabs of publicity as football, publicity it couldn't possibly afford to pay for at advertising rates. Yet no other sport provides less genuine information or indulges in more ludicrous secrecy about its affairs than soccer. Certainly no other sport clamps down so fiercely on officials or performers who dare to speak their minds honestly.

What can be done about it?

Plenty.

It's futile to try to make changes in the rules of the game, which have stood the test of time. It's not the actual game which is wrong; it's the style, the lack of top-class performers, the disinclination of so many to play attractive, attacking football.

It's futile to talk about three divisions. Indeed, it's far too late. Too many fans have left the game—and they'll never come back.

Perhaps success, too, is an unfair price to pay. Look at the clubs who take the honours today. They're princes only for a day. The fans look for even more success. A League flag, for instance, isn't enough. You've got to win the European Cup to continue to be the darlings of your supporters. Yes, success has probably more penalties than failure. Brutally, what's the difference between playing in the lower

A CURE FOR SICK SOCCER...
Manager Jock Stein of Celtic
feels amalgamation of clubs
would help.

half of the First Division and the top half of the Second? None. The crowds are about the same, the standard of play little different.

But something can be done—though I don't expect that it will. For it will hurt the pride of clubs who feel they must have a place in the football sun at all costs.

Undoubtedly the only way Scottish football can flourish in the future is by a measure of amalgamation.

Take Fife, for instance. How can a county with a population of less than 100,000 support East Fife, Dunfermline, Raith Rovers and Cowdenbeath? Wouldn't it be sensible to amalgamate them all and hope for a gate of around 12,000, county loyalty and the pick of the Fife players? Of course, it would. But will it ever happen?

Never. But what a real challenge we might have if Ayrshire, Lanarkshire and Renfrewshire also cut down to one club each. There are just not enough people to go round 37 clubs.

Celtic manager Jock Stein is one of the leading supporters of amalgamation. He puts it this way:

'Comparing Scotland with England is farcical. England has a much bigger population and there isn't nearly as big a gulf between their teams as there is here.

'Four up and four down has been suggested. With respect to the clubs concerned, how would, say, Clyde, Dunfermline, Stirling Albion and Queen of the South help the First Division any more than Airdrie, Kilmarnock, Dumbarton and Falkirk?'

'Amalgamation seems to me to be the only answer. But amalgamation must be in the interests of the big as well as the small clubs. The SFA and the League could help.'

And Stein pointed out that last season

A CURE FOR SICK SOCCER—
more outstanding personalities
like Celtic's Dixie Deans
might bring back the fans.

Celtic played Dundee United at Tannadice on the same day that Dundee travelled to play Rangers at Ibrox. 'I'm sure a lot of Dundonians would have liked to have seen both games. So why play them on the same day? It wouldn't be difficult to adjust the fixtures for separate Saturdays.

'There are other examples of this—too many crowd-pulling fixtures on the same day. This leaves other Saturdays less attractive. Why couldn't the potentially good games be spaced out when the fixtures are drawn up?'

In the end, I visualise football as a more compact organisation. Fewer teams but better teams. Football played inside huge plastic domes impervious to the weather, with the new artificial turf. Every ground almost a country club with first-class facilities—and entertainment for all the family. Less domestic competitions—and more glamorous clubs from abroad. Perhaps matches on Sundays.

A soccer Utopia? I'm afraid it's only a dream.

Meanwhile, something must be done to lift the apathy and give a lift of excitment and surge of interest to our most cherished sport.

People want better value for their money. The blunt truth is that, despite all the excuses, the fans don't fancy the current style and quality of the game. There is professional competence in many cases. That's not enough. There are not enough emergent personalities, too few Derek Johnstones, John Brownlies or Ken Dalgleish's.

We could also do with a longer summer break. There is a surfeit of soccer.

Can we take a lesson from English cricket? County cricket slumped dismally and there was panic. There was also a cure. It had nothing to do with tinkering with the laws of the game or the desperate cries for 'brighter cricket'.

The magic formula which brought a great upsurge of interest in cricket stemmed from a concentration on essentials—an international competition, on slimming the County Championships to 20 matches, on a spread of interest into varied but relevant club competition.

Scottish soccer should assimilate some of these lessons fast. The home internationals have been degraded to a weary appendage to the season's end, the League programme remains too long and too exacting.

The drum is no longer distant and the falling figures of attendance beat out the message too loud and clear to be ignored any longer.

104   A CURE FOR SICK SOCCER—
an end to the transfer south of stars such as Willie Johnston, of Rangers, seen here after the Ibrox club won the European Cup-winners Cup in Spain and before he left to join West Bromwich Albion.

The long trip I'll never forget

by Brian Third, Montrose

IF I EVER get round to having business cards printed, the motto would have to read . . . Have Boots, Will Travel.

I have never had any call or inclination to leave my home town of Fraserburgh, which means, as long as I am a Montrose player, a home game requires a round trip of 170 miles.

And, to take it to the other extreme, our annual League match at Stranraer means two full days away from home and a mileage approaching 540.

But that trip to Stranraer is one I would gladly make every weekend of my football career because of what happened at Stair Park last season.

I scored all six Montrose goals in our 6–3 victory. Talk about a journey being worth while.

Obviously, I remember this game better than most I have played with Montrose since my transfer from Highland League club Peterhead.

I remember, for instance, that I was certain after the first 10 minutes that I was going to have a real shocker. Nothing went right for me. I miskicked practically every time I went for the ball . . . and fell over it a few times, too.

Then, for no reason I can explain, everything started to go my way. Every time I hit the ball it seemed to end up in the Stranraer net.

By half time I had four goals, and,

during the interval, one of my team mates bet me a pound I wouldn't get six. Well, I almost didn't make it. I didn't score my sixth until the last minute.

I was so pleased I didn't bother to collect my bet, but I do have one souvenir of that game which I'll keep all my life.

A few weeks later, Stranraer showed what sportsmanship is all about by sending me the ball I had put in their net six times.

It was autographed by their players—even the goalkeeper—and now it is one of my most prized possessions.

Obviously, that game at Stranraer is the one I'll remember best of all from last season. But, as far as the club is concerned, the game they will recall with pride is the one I want to forget.

I am talking about our Scottish Cup fifth round replay against Hamilton at Douglas Park.

Eric Smith had become the highest-paid manager in the Second Division when he joined Accies a few weeks earlier, and since his arrival they had been going great guns in the League.

The first game, at Links Park, finished 2–2, although I think everyone agreed that Montrose should have finished the tie without the need for a replay.

Still, we had been playing so well away from home that we didn't worry unduly about the prospect of facing the replay . . . until yours truly took a hand.

105

Six minutes before the interval we were awarded a penalty when a header by big Ian Thomson was handled on the line. I had scored a few penalties earlier in the season, so I took this one . . . and rattled the ball off the crossbar.

A minute after half time the ball was again handled in the Hamilton penalty area and again the referee pointed to the spot.

I felt this was my chance to make up for the earlier miss. I tried to place the second spot-kick and this time the 'keeper saved.

Two penalty misses. How I wished the ground would open up and take me away. Quite honestly, I felt like walking off the pitch and right out of football.

I don't have to tell you how I felt when Harry Johnston finally scored the only goal of the replay with just eight minutes left. It was like having a 10-ton weight lifted off my shoulders.

That victory took Montrose into their first Scottish Cup quarter-final for 25 years, and, although we lost 4–1 to Dundee, I would have kicked myself all the way back to Fraserburgh if my penalty misses had cost us that glamour game!

(Brian Third is now with St. Mirren.)

Hard-hitting Brian Third, Montrose centre-forward, shows how he gets those vital goals.

The keeper who signed for a Scottish club in Belgium

by Thomson Allan, Dundee

N E X T time you want to set your pals a soccer poser, just ask them if any well-known Scottish player ever signed for his club in Belgium.

Chances are they'll say 'No' and you will be able to clean up on any bets they've dared to make. Because it was in Belgium that I became a Dundee player.

It all began when big Ally Donaldson went into dispute with the club on the eve of their pre-season trip to France and Belgium in 1971.

John Prentice, then manager of Dundee, was forced to start the tour with only one goalkeeper, Mike Hewitt. Before leaving Scotland, however, he started the negotiations that eventually made me his player.

And so, a couple of days later, I found myself on a jet bound for Brussels and on the way to beginning the best spell of my entire career.

I teamed up with the rest of the party at the resort town of Blankenberge and a few minutes later I was a Dundee player. Signed in the manager's hotel room overlooking the beach.

The then Dens Park boss's move for me ended the bleakest spell of my life, a spell which, at one time, looked like ending my days in football.

It began when it became clear that Gordon Marshall and Roy Baines were the first and second choices at Easter Road. I was reserve for the reserve side.

Thomson Allan, Dundee goalkeeper

(*Overleaf*) The man who taught Thomson Allan the finer arts of goalkeeping—Gordon Marshall, man of many clubs

Naturally, I wasn't happy with the situation and let Hibs know about it by asking for a transfer. But no one seemed to want me . . . not even Hibs. They gave me a free transfer at the end of season 1970–71.

By a strange twist—there are a few of these in this game—I might still have been a Hibs player if certain events hadn't happened in the order they did.

Soon after I was freed Eddie Turnbull, still with Aberdeen at that time, made an inquiry about taking me to Pittodrie.

Before he could follow it up, Dundee had moved in and signed me. Then, as everyone now knows, Eddie left the side he had built so successfully at Pittodrie to become manager at Easter Road.

I suppose that had Mr Turnbull moved earlier—before the end of the season I was freed by Hibs—he would have decided that I still had a part to play with Hibs.

However, the one thing you don't do in football is live on what might have been. And let me say here and now that my move to Dens Park was a great success.

Not immediately, of course. In that first season Mike Hewitt played so well that he

earned an Under-23 cap and Ally Donaldson settled his differences. It wasn't easy for me to make my mark with these two great 'keepers around—and once again I was third choice.

Then a couple of things happened to swing things my way. Ally was transferred to Falkirk and I was given my chance in pre-season friendlies against Preston and Crystal Palace.

I must have impressed Davie White, the new Dundee boss, because I suddenly found myself in the first team for the start of the season.

And I would like to thank two men for the part I played in what must go down as a pretty good season for Dundee and Thomson Allan.

No. 1, despite the fact that he helped end my days at Easter Road, was Gordon Marshall.

When he arrived at Easter Road as a vastly experienced goalkeeper I must admit I was little more than average. Gordon taught me all the finer points of the job, how a goalkeeper can become part of the unit that goes to make a successful side.

No. 2 is Davie White, the boss who gave me that big chance. He wasn't a 'keeper himself as a player but he certainly appreciates the problems that go with the job.

For instance, when I first became a senior, there was absolutely no special attention given to goalkeepers. They just did everything the rest of the lads did in training.

Davie White changed all that . . . and made me a much better goalkeeper. He realised that 'keepers didn't have to do the same work in training as outfield players.

He devised special training programmes and most of the good games I have had since have been thanks to that.

Thomson Allan had a spell with Hibernian before joining up at Dens Park. Here he is in action as the Easter Road 'keeper

How to turn on the style
Big crowds are the answer
by Jackie Copland, Dundee United

GOLF . . . tennis . . . cricket . . . football. I've tried most sports at some time or other in my life—but I have very definitely decided now that football is my game.

It wasn't always that way and I am certain that there were Dundee United supporters in my early days at Tannadice who would have advised me to stick to some other sport.

When I signed for United from Stranraer in December, 1970, I had been scor-

Jackie Copland, the man who is now a great defender for Dundee United, was once a noted goal-scorer with Stranraer, whose club tie he is adjusting here

ing goals regularly with the Second Division club.

So I went straight into the Tannadice first team as a striker—and became an almost overnight FAILURE.

I say almost because I did succeed in scoring against Hibs at Easter Road in my second or third game. After that, however, the goals simply dried up.

It was just one of those things a footballer cannot explain. One day you have the ability to score goals, the next it seems to desert you.

I did pick up the odd goal but I knew I wasn't hitting the back of the net regularly enough to justify the fee United had paid for me.

And so I finally found myself no longer sure of a first team place, even though United were going through a sticky patch.

Then, in November, 1971, Jerry Kerr stepped down after a long and successful career as manager to become general manager with United.

Jim McLean arrived at Tannadice and, although I didn't know it at the time, that brought about a big change for me.

Again, it didn't happen overnight. For a few months I was still in and out of the first team . . . still looking for the goal touch that had deserted me.

Then, at the end of a training session in January, the new boss came to me and asked how I would feel about becoming a defender.

I told him that I had, in fact, been a wing-half with Beith, my junior club, before going to Stranraer . . . and I told him I was willing to have a go at anything which might help my game.

We decided to work on it, first in practice matches, then a closed-door friendly against Dunfermline and finally a Dewar Shield tie against Peterhead.

And, from these small beginnings came Jackie Copland the defender, a new-look player many Tannadice supporters didn't recognise from the guy who used to break their hearts in the forward-line.

A couple of things made the transformation easy. Firstly, I reckon it is easier to play well at the back when you already have the experience of playing up front.

I was able to read the game quickly and go about stopping opponents with some authority

Secondly, I had some good players around me in the United defence, and it wasn't long before I fitted in alongside skipper Doug Smith. That wouldn't be hard for anyone, because Doug is such a good player—and such a cool customer that he makes everything look so simple.

The one game that sticks out in my mind particularly last season was our 1–0 victory over Hibs at Tannadice.

The Easter Road side were going great guns at the time, blasting four or five goals into opposing nets just about every week.

We knew the big danger was Alan Gordon, the player who had left United a year earlier and become the most lethal striker in the land. But we played him out of the game that day, just as we played the whole Hibs team out of the game.

Several times last season, United really turned on the style against the top teams. Our 2–2 draw with Celtic at Tannadice was another example.

The reason for this is simple, I think. Players find extra enthusiasm and extra reserves when they go out to tackle a strong side in front of a big crowd. It isn't easy to do that when you can count the fans on the terracings.

I am certain people south of the border would stop knocking Scottish football if our sides were able to play in front of the big crowds they get in England.

The mystery of the season

Fans are bewildered

IT TURNED into the *cause célèbre* of the season—and what a fuss it caused.

Few of the big crowd at Parkhead on 17 March, for the exciting Scottish Cup quarter-final between Celtic and Aberdeen, saw anything untoward.

But a linesman did—and so once again referee Bobby Davidson, most controversial official in the game, was the object of the fury of the Old Firm fans.

It seemed that Jimmy Johnstone, of Celtic, and Jim Hermiston, of Aberdeen, had a brush when the ball was away. The eagle-eyed linesman waved to attract the attention of the referee.

A consultation—then the referee talked to both players. Hermiston was booked—and, to a roar of astounded fury from the crowd, off went Johnstone.

Apparently, Hermiston had been tugging Johnstone's jersey—and the Celtic winger had tried too energetically, in the view of the linesman, to get free.

But all ended well. When Johnstone's case was heard by the SFA Referee, the Celt was dismissed without a stain on his character.

Nevertheless, the incident didn't add to the popularity of Mr. Davidson with the Celtic supporters.

Here's the drama in pictures:

It looks all rather inocuous just the start of another
series of bookings. Jimmy Johnstone, the linesman and
Jim Hermiston are grim as the name of the Aberdeen
back goes into the notebook of referee Davidson.

Consternation! Johnstone can't
believe it. He has been ordered
off.

Angry Celtic colleagues argue
with the referee, ask him to
change his mind. Not a chance.

And off runs Johnstone with
Bobby Murdoch offering
consolation.

Another time, another place—
but the same old drama. Referee
Davidson orders off John
Blackley following an incident
with a linesman at Ibrox.

Black day in Budapest
Class—the top priority in the European Cup

CLASS. Class, culture, confidence. That's what football's really all about. Two players with class, culture and confidence and you don't have to worry about fancy formations, dour drill or robot rule. Two players with style and you can wave a happy farewell to 4–2–4's and 4–3–3's.

I am more and more coming to the conclusion that football, as always, will flourish only when there are world class players around. Success at the top level arrives when a team has more outstanding players than the rest. This has been proved in recent years.

I am not going into an argument about whether a team of 11 class players would beat a side based on the method style, with the accent on hard graft and work-rate. I think they would—but it's a matter of opinion.

Of what I am convinced is that to win World or European Cups a team must have first at least two stars who combine the elegance of the masters of yesteryear with the venom and stamina of a Cruyff—and then a stern defensive method and solid supporting players for the top-of-the-bill duo.

But I'd settle for two great stars gifted with the airs and graces of what, at its best, used to be an art rather than worry about finding players to fit into a supporting method.

What, you may say, about Manchester United, who had more shining stars than most but faded sadly in season 1972–73, and went back, indeed, to a fierce fighting style?

It's hardly fair to suggest that United's dependence on great forward talents brought them to the disaster area.

Some pundits allege that United failed because they did not have enough method, failed to use a 'support play' technique. This means having team-mates near enough to pass to, providing the player in possession of the ball with alternative, making progress through the efforts of a squad rather than the genius of one.

In short, United are condemned for not having supporting players to run off the ball. Too many United players, said the critics, merely wanted the ball, did not want to help a mate. A case of too many chiefs and not enough Indians?

Perhaps. Or perhaps not. In the good old days, United's football was successful because they had based their tactics on sound defenders behind great attacking players and the only plan necessary was to get the ball to Charlton, Law or Best.

That, in my opinion, is what really went wrong with United. Law and Charlton aged, Best lost the place. I'll be so bold as to suggest that if United today had players as outstanding as Law, Best and Charlton were in their heyday they wouldn't have to concentrate on the new tactical grammar of the game and would still be at the top.

And there's the rub. Where nowadays do you find two, never mind three, players of world class calibre?

This, I feel, is what Celtic must do now if they are ever again to become the best

Oh, they do like to be beside the seaside, do Celtic. Their favourite training headquarters before big matches is down at Seamill, on the Ayrshire coast. Here they are in good spirits as they take a run along the beach.

team in Europe and prove it by winning the European Cup.

The lesson was rubbed home to them on a sad November afternoon in Budapest when they were turfed out of Europe's premier competition by Ujpest Dosza.

Some Celtic fans moaned about defensive blunders. Others felt the 3–0 defeat was caused because Celtic used wrong tactics.

But the truth was that the Hungarians won because they had in Ferenc Bene and Antol Dunai two magnificent players, two players who had the craft of Mason, James and Gallagher, two players who would have shone in any company on the soccer globe.

Celtic did not have one of that calibre.

I insist . . . in the 1970's the recipe for success has as its principal ingredient the inclusion of at least two players who can sew a thread of gold through solid efficiency.

Ajax prove it, with Cryuff and Keiser. So do all the other top teams, especially at international level with West Germany, who have many more class players than Beckenbauer and Netzer.

122

But, some may say, didn't Celtic win the European Cup with a striking display of aggressive football, with pace and hard graft the theme, in Lisbon?

Sure, and I wrote that Celtic became kings of Europe in 1967 by beating Inter Milan 2–1 mainly because of their hurricane attacking.

But I also pointed out that manager Jock Stein had set a new pattern—method plus *magic*. And the magic came from players who, on that wonderful Lisbon day, were of world class—Auld, Johnstone and Gemmell. Not to mention Bobby Murdoch. They were the men who supplied the magic, the cunning and the dash. The others, of course, did splendidly, supplying the support and the method.

Looking back, however, it is obvious that Celtic really won because they had more really class players than Inter.

And it will always be this way in the European Cup.

Nowadays Celtic are in a transitional period. Now and again they burst into fiery action. They are still, in my view, the best side in Scotland, although competition, especially from Hibernian and Rangers, is growing fiercer. But Bobby Murdoch, though still a fine middle-man, is growing older, Auld and Gemmell have gone, Jimmy Johnstone doesn't turn on his entrancing soccer as often as he once did.

And although Celtic often turn on the style they haven't—and certainly hadn't against Ujpest—a player who can stake a claim for a place in a World Class XI.

Young Kenny Dalglish may attain the heights for he has all the potential. But Celtic need someone like Bertie Auld, a player of craft and cunning and magical touches.

Well done, mate. Celtic's Dixie Deans and Jim Brogan congratulate each other after another win.

Celtic, of course, will go on trying to be emperors of Europe again. I feel, however, they will not succeed in their aim until they find another player of the same class as Dalglish.

In George Connelly, of course, they have an elegant star. But Connelly weaves his spells from behind. For success in Europe it's class up front that matters most.

And yet . . . and yet. It might have been all so different for Celtic in the European Cup last season if it hadn't been for injury —and defensive slips.

Bobby Murdoch was unfit for the first leg on October 25 at Parkhead. So was the experienced Jim Brogan.

And things went wrong at Parkhead. They went wrong mainly because of the genius of Bene.

The pattern had been predictable. Celtic hammering into ferocious attack. The Hungarians suavely defending—but looking dangerous on the break.

In 20 minutes there was tragedy. Ujpest scored a beautifully taken goal, a gem of opportunism. Eddy Dunai sent a long ball through the middle. The ball soared over the head of Celtic centre-half Billy McNeill and Bene controlled it beautifully, went on, lured Evan Williams from his goal and hit the ball perfectly into the net.

Kenny Dalglish, that great prospect, scored two goals to put Celtic 2–1 up by the end—but the writing was on the ball. The thoughtful realised two goals against the menacing Ujpest wouldn't be enough.

There was hope, of course, when Celtic flew out for the second leg early in November in the grey city of Budapest by the brown Danube. There's always hope when Celtic play. That's why they have such a fantastic record.

But, alas, only hope . . .

And there was to be no repeat of the epic victory in the European Cup of the previous year. That's when Hungarian papers said of Celtic's 2–1 win over Ujpest in the first leg in Budapest:

'No football team anywhere in the world would be able to stand its ground against Glasgow Celtic in a match like last night's when, playing with great gusto, they beat Ujpest Dozsa.

'Celtic are a tough, well disciplined and well balanced side, with stamina and go. They had superior technique, teamwork, skills and speed.'

Ujpest had learned their lessons from that game. They never gave Celtic a chance. And Bene and Antol Dunai were superb players who strolled to victory.

Perhaps Celtic would have done better if Bobby Murdoch had been fit for Celtic lacked the midfield composure absolutely vital against a team of Ujpest's class. They had no one to direct the traffic, a job Murdoch does so efficiently.

There was another aspect, of course, which is seldom mentioned. The aspect of practice in defence. Celtic are seldom required to defend in Scotland and so when deep defence become mandatory in Europe the tactical switch must be comprehensive. So Celtic often seem lost when they have to play in the Inter Milan manner.

That was obvious in Budapest for Celtic's defensive nervousness was glaring, even among the old hands, and Bene and Dunai took full advantage. Indeed, if it hadn't been for the brilliance of Williams, so often criticised by the fans, Celtic might have been humiliated.

And what a sad season this early defeat in Europe meant for so many Scots, who relish the torrid European Cup.

The matches in the Spring against the pick of Europe bring much-needed

That's a relief, says elegant George Connelly as he watches Celtic skipper, Billy McNeil, clear the lines in a tough match against Rangers.

125

How tough is it to play against the happy Celts? This picture tells you. What a scramble there is in the Ayr United goalmouth as Celtic storm into attacking action

glamour to a Scottish soccer scene which is far from bright.

Maybe we expect too much from Celtic. But they are not through as a force in Europe, though they may have to consolidate and experiment, change and buy before they challenge for the top cup again.

After all, they have a tremendous record in the European Cup. They went out in the first round in 1967, four months after they had won the cup, to Dynamo Kiev, but since then they have been in another final and a semi-final.

Celtic's two matches against Ujpest Dozsa brought their total number of games played in the European Cup to 44.

Ahead of them are Real Madrid, and Benfica, AC Milan have also played 44 and just below Celtic are Manchester United, with 41. And, naturally, Ajax, the new wonders of Europe, are fast becoming experienced European Cup campaigners, having competed more than 40 times.

Celtic's qualification for the European Cup for the seventh successive time made them Britain's leading club in the foremost tournament. The season before they equalled the record of six appearances which had been held by Rangers. The only other British club coming near this record is Manchester United, who have appeared in five competitions.

Make no mistake. The European Cup is still the big one, the competition every club most wants to play in, the most exciting and important of them all.

It's 18 years since a French journalist, Gabriel Hanot, presented L'Equipe, the sporting paper, with the idea for the tournament. And in 1955-56 the European Cup was begun.

Hanot's plan was to combine the Mitropa Cup, inaugurated in Central Europe in 1927 for competition among

Austria, Italy, Czechoslovakia, Hungary and Yugoslavia, and the Latin Cup, started in 1949 for the champion clubs of France, Spain, Italy and Portugal, with the top clubs in Western and Northern Europe also being invited.

In 1955-56, 17 countries were represented but Chelsea, under pressure from the English Football League, withdrew. The English saw the tournament as a threat to their competition. Hibernian were the first British club to play in the new tournament and reached the semifinal in 1955-56, losing to Rheims, who had the great Kopa in their team. As I said, you need the world class stars for success!

The following season Manchester United became the first English club to participate.

The competition was dominated for the first 11 years by Spanish, Portuguese and Italian clubs and it wasn't until 1967 that Scotland gained the trophy, thanks to Celtic's victory over Inter-Milan.

Now the Dutch dominate the tournament, with Ajax the top team.

Let's hope Celtic are back on European Cup business soon.

And let's hope even more they find the stars of the quality I've described to give them the winning formula.

The picture that says it all. When Celtic score . . . well, they celebrate like this